A Mapuche homestead

OCCASIONAL CONTRIBUTIONS FROM THE MUSEUM OF
ANTHROPOLOGY OF THE UNIVERSITY OF MICHIGAN
NO. 15

ARAUCANIAN CULTURE IN TRANSITION

BY
MISCHA TITIEV

ANN ARBOR
UNIVERSITY OF MICHIGAN PRESS
1951

To my mother

PREFACE

THE project described in this monograph was first planned early in 1941. In that year support was received from the Board of Governors of the Horace H. Rackham School of Graduate Studies and a leave of absence was obtained from the University of Michigan. After preliminary plans for field work had been completed, America's entry into World War II brought about a delay of several years in carrying out the program.

In January, 1948, I was fortunate enough to secure a sabbatical leave from the University of Michigan and an additional grant of funds from the Board of Governors of the Horace H. Rackham School of Graduate Studies. Accompanied by my wife I left for Chile at the end of the month and arrived in Santiago on February 19, 1948. Here we met Mr. Raúl González Mella, a doctoral candidate in geography at the University of Chile, who had previously agreed to serve as a field assistant. After two weeks spent in visiting museums and libraries and conferring with various scholars in Santiago, we entrained for Temuco, capital of Cautín province, in the heart of the Indian-inhabited territory still known as the Frontera (Map 1).

Many students have expressed such lively curiosity about the methods used by an anthropologist in locating a specific field station and in making initial contact with native informants that a short statement of the procedure followed in this instance may not be amiss.

Before we left the United States, it was learned from anthropologists conversant with Chile that the Reverend Dillman S. Bullock was one of the best informed men on Araucanian matters in that country. An exchange of letters brought a cordial invitation to visit Mr. Bullock at the famed agricultural station called El Vergel, in Angol. He received us on March 4, 1948, and advised us to plan to work in the neighborhood of Cholchol, to get in touch with members of the Anglican Misión Araucana stationed at Quepe and Cholchol (Map 2), and to bear in mind the possibility of using as our first informant the Reverend Juan Antinao, an Araucanian who is an ordained Episcopal clergyman.

Acting on Mr. Bullock's advice, we next called on Canon and Mrs. William Wilson at Quepe. They agreed that Cholchol was the most suitable center for ethnological investigation, and Mrs. Wilson graciously offered to loan us her caravan (a small, ox-drawn trailer; see Pl. III, Fig. 1), which was destined to serve as our home for the greater part of our stay in Chile.

A few days later, on March 10, we met the Reverend Harry Donaldson, chief of the Misión Araucana, who promptly invited us to visit his home and station in Cholchol. Through the active and friendly co-operation of Mr. and Mrs. Donaldson and their staff, we succeeded in equipping the caravan for winter use, in having it drawn to the field, and in concluding arrangements to work with the Reverend Juan Antinao at his home reduction of Cautinche.

After making several studies in and around Cholchol during the remainder of March we took up residence at Cautinche on April 5 and remained there until May 10. We then had the caravan taken to Carrarriñe, where we stayed, except for a two-week trip to Santiago, until July 17. After that, the caravan was drawn into Cholchol, and we were given the privilege of using the mission house as a base while we made an investigation of Renaco (Map 2). We left Cholchol for Temuco on July 27 and concluded our visit to Chile on August 10, 1948, after working for ten days in Santiago.

Many people have contributed to the successful accomplishment of the project. I am thankful to all who have aided me, whether or not their names are specifically mentioned. To the Board of Governors of the Horace H. Rackham School of Graduate Studies, and to the Board of Regents of the University of Michigan, I am deeply grateful for generous support and for the sabbatical leave. Thanks are also due Dr. Donald D. Brand, Dr. Junius B. Bird, Dr. Julian H. Steward, and Sister M. Inez Hilger, who helped me formulate my field plans before departing for Chile; Dr. Eugenio Pereira, Dr.

Ricardo Donoso, Dr. Humberto Fuenzalida, and Dr. Leopoldo Pizarro (all of Santiago), for much useful advice pertaining to my program of work; the Reverend Mr. Bullock for directing us to the Misión Araucana and Cholchol; and Canon and Mrs. Wilson for many helpful suggestions and the loan of the caravan.

Among the most helpful Araucanian informants were Juan Antinao, his wife Aurora, and his daughter Josephina at Cautinche; Segundo Paineo, Domingo Carilaf, and Fermín Collío at Carrarriñe; Segundo Huenchual and Fermín Nahuelhual at Renaco; J. M. Collío Huaiquilaf at Santiago; and Ramón Chihuaicura, whose guest I was at a *ñillatun* ceremony at Coigue.

To Raúl González I owe many thanks for his cheerful acceptance of numerous inconveniences in the field, for his assistance in conducting interviews and securing data in Spanish, and for his drawings of most of the maps and figures reproduced in this work. For further assistance with maps and figures I am particularly indebted to Mary Walfred Stauch and to William M. Masters; I am grateful also to Gertrude D. Stevens and to Edith M. Todter for typing the entire manuscript.

I wish to thank James T. Babb and David H. Clift, director and associate director of the Yale University Library, for providing excellent working facilities in the summer of 1949, and the members of the Yale faculty who favored me with their advice while this monograph was being prepared. Dr. Samuel K. Lothrop was kind enough to read my manuscript and to contribute many valuable suggestions that have been incorporated in the final draft. Dr. James B. Griffin, director of the Museum of Anthropology, University of Michigan, has shown a continuous interest in the project, and I am grateful for his co-operation in making arrangements for the publication of the manuscript.

To my wife I am deeply indebted, particularly for her willingness to spend a Chilean winter in the field, for her help in establishing contacts with the natives and gathering information, and for keeping house in the caravan until she left for the United States late in May. I have also had the benefit of her advice and criticism in the preparation of this report.

Above all, the field trip could not have accomplished its objectives without the unselfish friendship and help of the Reverend and Mrs. Harry Donaldson and the staff of the Misión Araucana. Their experience in dealing with Chileans and natives was constantly employed on our behalf, and their unfailing willingness to assist us in every possible way contributed much toward making our stay in Chile a memorable and pleasant experience.

CONTENTS

ILLUSTRATIONS

PLATES

(Plates I–XVI follow page 164)

FIGURES IN THE TEXT

MAPS

INTRODUCTION

Selection of the Araucanians as subjects for research in the field was by no means a matter of chance. On the contrary, they were chosen because they represent a large and important tribe of South American Indians about whom there is a surprising lack of up-to-date information. In the course of the last four centuries a great deal of valuable material on numerous phases of their culture has been written by soldiers, travelers, scholars, and missionaries, but this monograph provides the first ethnographic report ever compiled from data gathered in the field by a professional anthropologist.[1] It would be presumptuous to claim, on the basis of a single field trip, that one had made adequate coverage of the total range of Araucanian culture; hence a word of explanation is necessary to indicate the area covered, the native groupings, the limitations of time, and the problems and objectives presented in this study.

First, the area will be considered. Approximately three hundred miles south of Santiago, from the Río Bío Bío, an eighty-mile wide stretch of territory extends about one hundred and fifty miles farther south. Most of this region is a valley contained between the Nahuelbuta coastal range on the west and the Andean mountains on the east. The area has long been known as the Frontera (Map 1) because it is beyond the system of forts erected by the Spaniards during the conquest of Chile. Commonly, this territory is called Araucanía, because it is the principal zone inhabited by the Araucanian Indians. At present native communities are scattered over much of the old Fron-

[1] Compare the statement of this situation in Brand (1941*a*, p. 29), whose work provides the most complete bibliography of Araucanian studies that is readily available. The late Father Cooper's excellent summary of the existing literature (Cooper, 1946) will be frequently cited to indicate earlier treatments of topics covered in this monograph. It should be noted that in 1945 Sister M. Inez Hilger made a field study, principally centered on child-rearing practices, among several Araucanian groups. For a preliminary description of her findings, see Hilger, 1946. A full report is now in press.

For bibliographic references to works mentioned see Literature Cited.

tera. Not all of them have identical customs, and it is well known that important cultural differences exist between the indigenes residing north of the Cautín River and those living to the south of it.[2] This monograph deals only with the Araucanians north of the Cautín River, in the area bounded by Carrarriñe, Cautinche, Renaco, and Cholchol (Map 2).

There is no way of knowing at present when the aboriginal settlement of Araucanía took place, nor is there any precise way of determining the exact number of Araucanians extant. Statistics vary from official government figures of approximately one hundred thousand to unofficial estimates of three hundred thousand.[3] Part of the discrepancy may arise from the fact that there is no longer any clear indication of race by means of which one can distinguish a full-blooded Araucanian from a mestizo or a rural Chilean. Nor is it always easy to define an Araucanian in terms of culture. The best single test seems to be that of language. In fact, it has become customary to class as an Araucanian any person who habitually speaks the native tongue. Thus, Araucanian has come to refer not only to the language itself but also to one who speaks it. In their own speech, the Indians call themselves Mapuche ("people of the land"), and throughout this monograph the words Araucanian and Mapuche will be used interchangeably to signify either the aboriginal language or the natives who speak it.

There is a strong likelihood that a number of non-Araucanian peoples once lived in the territory under discussion. Various efforts have been made, notably by Guevara and Latcham, to identify these groups and to indicate their locations. The late Father Cooper reviewed and summarized all the available data, and recognized a number of distinctive regional or tribal subdivisions, such as the Picunche of northern middle Chile, the Mapuche and Huilliche of southern middle Chile, and the Pehuenche on the higher slopes of the Andes. Since most of these have been absorbed or exterminated, Cooper put the greatest emphasis on what is clearly the main surviving body

[2] Latcham, 1924, pp. 263 ff.

[3] Brand, 1941*a*, p. 24; and Cooper, 1946, p. 695.

of Araucanian speakers, whose culture he described under the term Mapuche-Huilliche.[4] This is the group with which my report is concerned.

To turn next to limitations of time, it is an accepted fact that the Araucanians were first brought within the scope of Euro-American history in 1536, when some of them met the Spanish forces led by Diego de Almagro. Soon after this, the permanent occupation of Araucanian territory was begun by Pedro de Valdivia, who founded Santiago in 1541 and within the next twelve years established cities and forts as far south as Valdivia. Properly speaking, then, the known history of the Mapuche extends over a span of four hundred years. This study does not propose to cover such a lengthy period. A brief historical sketch will be provided in the succeeding chapter, but I shall deal for the most part with the culture of the Araucanians after they were pacified in 1884, and more particularly with the situation that has arisen since 1917, when the practice of allotting lands in severalty began.

As far as problems and objectives are concerned, circumstances did not permit an unrestricted coverage. Accordingly, a program was adopted that seemed best suited to fill some of the widest gaps in the existing knowledge concerning the Mapuche. Among the most serious lacunae are those in the fields of kinship and sociopolitical organization. The unsatisfactory nature of the published material on these topics is highlighted by the fact that so conscientious and thorough a student as Father Cooper was forced to treat kinship in terms of a unit which, he stated, has been variously designated as *kuga*, *cuga*, *cüga*, *cunga*, and *elpa*, the use of which went out of existence between one hundred and one hundred and fifty years ago, no memory of which now survives, and which has been described or translated by no less than fourteen distinct Spanish or English terms.[5] Likewise, in dealing with sociopolitical culture,

[4] Further details regarding Chile's aboriginal population may be found in Latcham, 1924, pp. 258–74; Guevara, 1929, I: 191–259; and Cooper, 1946, pp. 687–99.

[5] Cooper, 1946, p. 722.

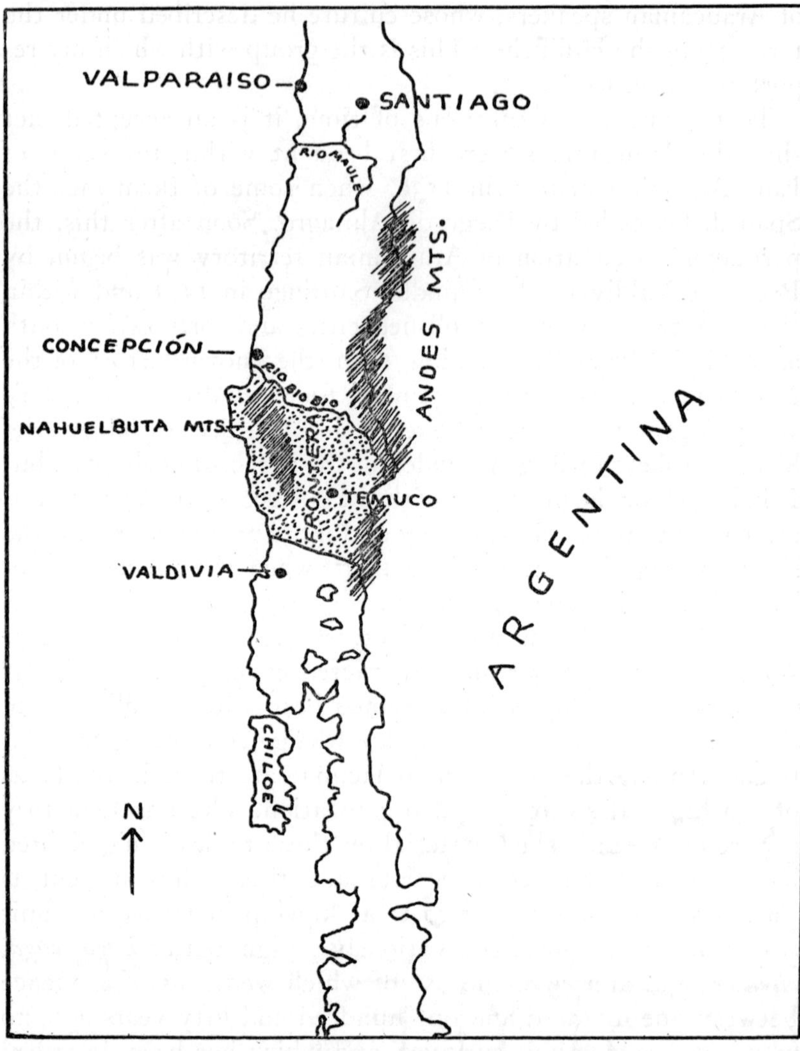

MAP 1. The Frontera in Chile. The stippled area gives the approximate location of the region called the Frontera or Araucanía. (After Jefferson, 1921, Figs. 6 and 13.)

Father Cooper was led to write: "Our sources are so vague and often so conflicting . . . that it is impossible to reconstruct therefrom a full, rounded, and consistent picture."[6]

[6] *Ibid.*, p. 724.

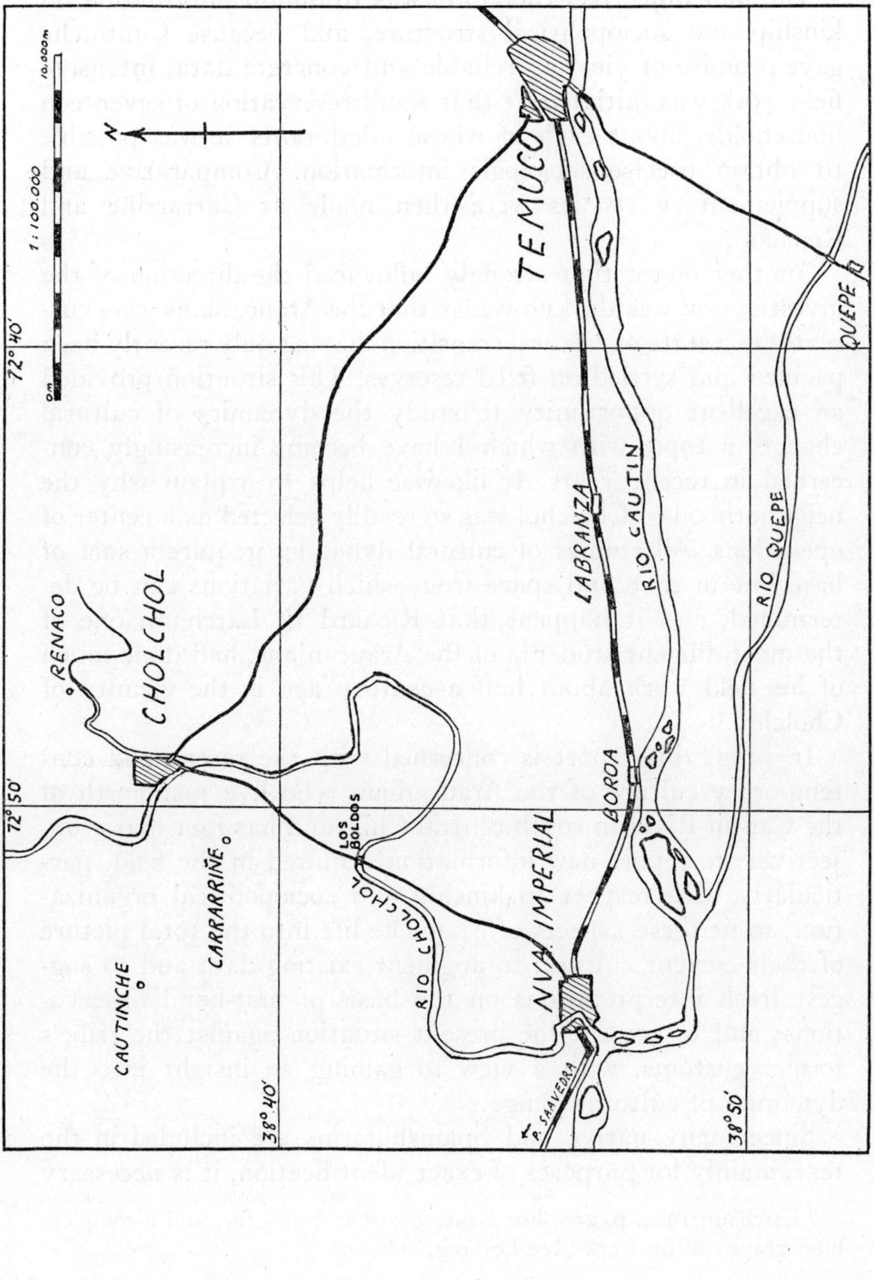

MAP 2. Cholchol and vicinity. Redrawn from an original sketch by Raúl González.

The first objective, therefore, was to obtain information on kinship and sociopolitical structure, and because Cautinche gave promise of yielding reliable and concrete data, intensive field work was initiated at that small reservation of seventeen households, about each of whose inhabitants it was possible to obtain precise sociologic information. Comparative and supplementary studies were then made at Carrarriñe and Renaco.

Another factor that strongly influenced the direction of the investigation was the knowledge that the Araucanians were currently in a state of cultural transition, having only recently been pacified and settled on fixed reserves. This situation provided an excellent opportunity to study the dynamics of cultural change, a topic with which I have become increasingly concerned in recent years. It likewise helps to explain why the neighborhood of Cholchol was so readily selected as a center of operations. All studies of cultural dynamics require a sort of base line in time and space from which variations can be determined, and it happens that Richard E. Latcham, one of the most diligent students of the Araucanians, had done much of his field work about half a century ago in the vicinity of Cholchol.[7]

In brief, this report is concerned with the recent and contemporary culture of the Araucanians who live just north of the Cautín River in south central Chile and has four major objectives: to report new information acquired in the field, particularly with respect to kinship and sociopolitical organization; to fit these aspects of Mapuche life into the total picture of their current culture; to augment existing data and to suggest fresh interpretations on the basis of first-hand observations; and to project the present situation against the tribe's former customs, with a view to gaining an insight into the dynamics of culture change.

Since many native and Spanish terms are included in the text, mainly for purposes of exact identification, it is necessary

[7] Latcham, 1924, p. 250. For a sketch of Latcham's life, and a complete bibliography of his works, see Lothrop, 1945.

to explain the system of transcription. Spanish words are given in their standard form, but Mapuche terms are rendered according to the method employed by Fray Félix José de Augusta,[8] with the following exceptions: inverted *e* will be represented by *u*, hooked *n* will be written as *ñ*, and elongated *s* will be given as *s*. The plurals of all Mapuche words will be made by the addition of *s*.

Before closing this introduction I wish to call attention to the great need for additional studies of Araucanian culture. Opportunities still exist for investigations both north and south of the Cautín River. In addition to whatever contributions may be made by the publication of this monograph, it is hoped that it will stimulate other anthropologists to exploit the rich potentialities for field research that yet remain among the Araucanians of Chile.

[8] Augusta, 1916.

HISTORICAL BACKGROUND

If one wishes to understand the process by which the contemporary situation of the Mapuche came into being, it is essential to know some of the salient aspects of their past. For that purpose an effort will be made to provide a historic outline that will include only those events which have had the greatest impact on the development of the tribe's culture.

Broadly speaking, Araucanian history may be divided into five parts: a pre-Spanish period before Almagro's arrival in Chile in 1536; the Spanish period, between 1536 and the establishment of the Chilean republic about 1810; the early decades of the republic, between 1810 and 1884; the era of pacification and settlement on reservations, from 1884 to 1917; and the time of the allotment program since 1917, featured by the allocation of land in severalty. It is with the last two periods that this monograph is primarily concerned.

PRE-SPANISH PERIOD, BEFORE 1536

Neither historians nor archeologists have yet been able to establish the date when Araucanians first settled in what is now called Chile,[1] nor does any one know the extent of the territory that they originally occupied. Events remain obscure until the middle of the fifteenth century, when the Araucanian domain was invaded from the north by the powerful Incas. During the struggle that followed the Mapuche were forced to yield some ground, but they seem to have been successful in establishing a frontier at the Río Maule (Map 1). No doubt the Incas sometimes penetrated far beyond the Maule, and their comings and goings unquestionably affected the lives and customs of the Chilean aborigines, yet it is generally agreed that the Incas met with such stubborn opposition that on the whole "the in-

[1] New light will certainly be shed on this topic when hitherto unpublished reports of excavations in the Cautín Valley become available. According to a note from Lothrop, Mapuche log coffins and unpainted pottery have been found stratified over stone box graves and painted pottery with Inca-influenced patterns.

fluence of the *Inca* culture upon Araucanian . . . does not appear to have been very profound."[2]

THE SPANISH PERIOD, 1536–1810

Araucanian contacts with Spaniards fall into two parts. The first, especially in the century between 1541 and 1641, was marked by savage and almost perpetual warfare. The second, from 1641 to 1810, was relatively less violent and consisted of stretches of peace, intermittently broken by bitter fighting.

Active warfare commenced in 1541, as soon as Pedro de Valdivia began his Chilean campaigns. His forces quickly overran the region between the Río Maule and the Río Bío Bío (Map 1), but Araucanian resistance intensified when the Spaniards tried to penetrate into the rainy and forested country south of the Bío Bío. The Mapuche, led by their great tribal heroes Lautaro and Caupolicán, whose exploits are celebrated in Ercilla's poem, *La Araucana*, simply would not acknowledge defeat and even succeeded in killing Valdivia in 1553. After many more years of continuous fighting, Spain finally recognized the independence of the Indians and concluded the pact of Quillín on January 9, 1641, in which the Bío Bío was formally recognized as the northern limit of Araucanian territory. Thereupon, the era of incessant fighting gradually came to an end, and until the Chilean war of independence began in 1810: "Spanish-Araucanian relationships consisted mainly of many guerilla raids . . . and numerous peace agreements. Only the uprisings of 1723 and 1766 were general."[3]

Despite their bloody opposition to the Spaniards, the Araucanians were strongly influenced by Spanish culture. In a succinct summary of this situation Latcham has written: "The Spanish conquest brought with it knowledge of new cereals and plants, other domestic animals [especially, horses and oxen], a fuller use of metals, and a considerable change in the tribal government, owing to the necessity of continued union to repel

[2] Cooper, 1946, p. 696. A strong dissent from the prevailing point of view is registered in Guevara, 1929, I: 143–87.

[3] Brand, 1941*a*, p. 19.

the invader."[4] Latcham also emphasized the devastating effects that resulted from the introduction of powerful spirituous liquors.

EARLY DECADES OF THE REPUBLIC, 1810–1884

It will be recalled that the pact of Quillín, in 1641, had formally established the Río Bío Bío as the northern frontier of Araucanian territory. Throughout the years that followed, and despite numerous violations of the arrangement by both sides, the Bío Bío continued to be regarded as the northern boundary of Araucanía, and this alignment was specifically confirmed by treaty at the date of Chilean independence.[5] Curiously enough, as Mark Jefferson pointed out, no southern border to Indian-held land was named in the treaty,[6] but Araucanía was unofficially understood to terminate at the latitude of Valdivia, where the forests end and open country begins. Thus, in the decade or so following 1810, while Chile was struggling to make good her drive for independence from Spain, the wooded area between the Bío Bío and Valdivia was left to the Araucanians. This was the stretch approximately one hundred and fifty miles in length that comprised Araucanía or the Frontera.

At about the same time that the formation of the Chilean republic was taking place, the long-continued resistance of the Mapuche to white encroachment began to decrease. This does not imply that no native revolts occurred after 1810, but it does suggest that after a record of nearly three hundred years of bitter fighting, even the most obdurate of the nineteenth-century Araucanians must have realized that they could not hope to eliminate their hated rivals. In addition, although the Mapuche still resisted any mass penetration of their region, they were becoming subjected to a new kind of unofficial infiltration. This was brought about by the entrance of Chilean squatters who were willing to risk their lives in the hope of improving their lot, and by the incursion of outlaws and despera-

[4] Latcham, 1909, p. 335.

[5] Jefferson, 1921, p. 29.

[6] *Ibid.* It was not until 1852 that the Toltén River was officially declared to be the southern limit of the Frontera.

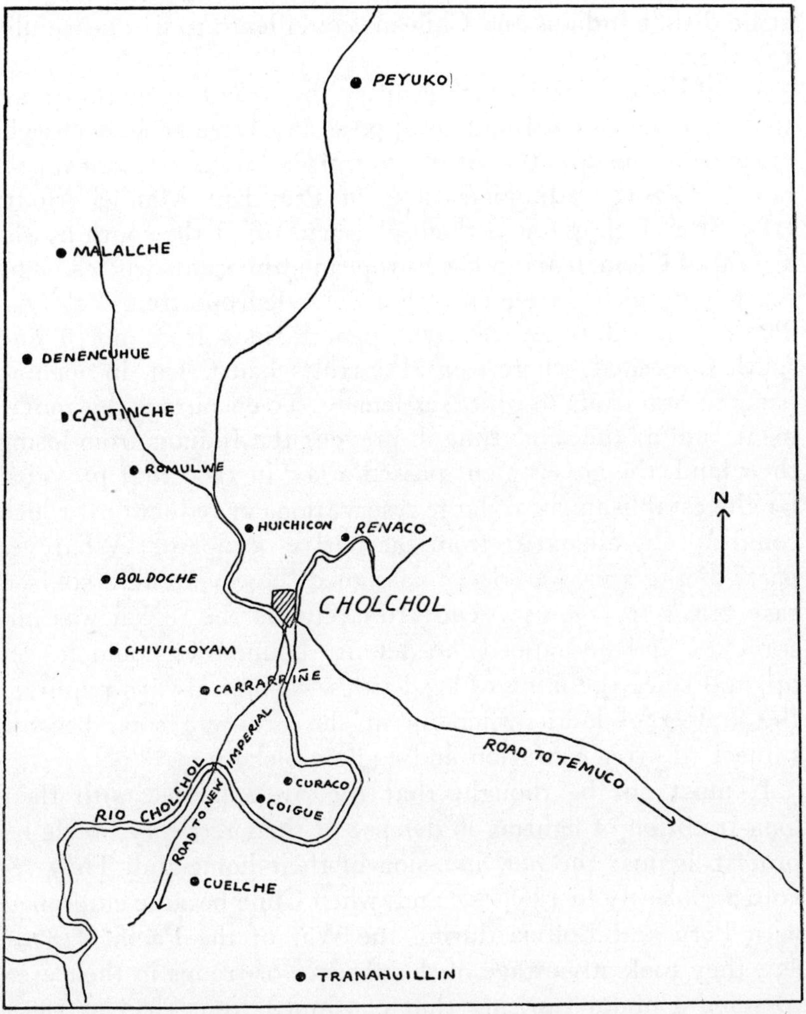

FIG. 1. Reservations near Cholchol. Redrawn from an original sketch loaned by the Reverend Harry Donaldson, of the Misión Araucana. Only reductions mentioned in the text are noted. They indicate the density of reserves around Cholchol. Locations are approximate.

does who sought refuge in the unpoliced sectors of the Frontera. Not all of these invaders were killed, and, in the course of time, some of them married Araucanian women and gradually demonstrated that Indians and Chileans could learn to live peacefully together.

Until the mid-nineteenth century the Araucanians continued to be on their guard and to oppose any large scale encroachment from the direction of the country's capital on their north, but during the administrations of President Manuel Montt (1851–1861), they found themselves cut off at the south by the arrival of German and other European immigrants who came by sea to establish settlements that extended out from Valdivia. Thereafter, relatively peaceful penetrations from north and south succeeded, where frontal assaults had failed, in opening parts of Araucanía to white settlement. To encourage this movement, and at the same time to prevent the Indians from losing their land, the government passed a law in 1866 that provided for the establishment of large reservations or reductions, which could not be alienated from the native occupants. Whatever parts of the area were left unassigned, however, were sold on easy terms to colonists. Unfortunately, as the region was unsurveyed and unmapped, no definite boundaries could be set up, and since the filing of legal titles was not always required, the matter of land ownership in the Frontera soon became subject to utter confusion and endless bickering.

It must not be thought that the Araucanians, with their long tradition of fighting in defense of their territory, made no protest against the new invasion of their homeland. They revolted violently in 1868–70; and, when Chile became embroiled with Peru and Bolivia during the War of the Pacific (1879–83), they took advantage of the absence of troops in their area to stage a major uprising that continued from 1880 to 1882. This turned out to be their last major effort to regain their lost independence. As soon as Chile began to feel assured of victory in the War of the Pacific, she sent her seasoned soldiers to the Frontera, with the result that by 1884 the Araucanians were thoroughly defeated and pacified.[7]

[7] Galdames, 1941, p. 337. Dr. Lothrop said that in Latcham's opinion the use of modern weapons was a decisive factor in the final defeat of the Araucanians.

PACIFICATION AND THE RESERVATION SYSTEM, 1884–1917

When the government of Chile, in the year following the victorious termination of the War of the Pacific, succeeded in pacifying the Araucanians, it took the stand that the Mapuche deserved to be punished for their disloyalty in revolting while the country was at war. Accordingly, it was decreed that the titles to their tribal reservations were to be cancelled, and their holdings were declared state property.[8] The Indians were permitted to remain on the reservations previously set aside for them, but all of Araucanía was politically subdivided to form several of the present provinces including Bío Bío, Malleco, and Cautín. In fact, it was upon the establishment of the last-named province in 1887 that "the whole of the Frontera was incorporated in the organized national domain,"[9] and to all intents and purposes the Araucanians thereafter became an ethnic minority group of Chilean citizens living within the borders of the republic. New towns and cities sprang up all about them, lines of communication crossed and recrossed their former territory, roads and railroads were built throughout the region, and within a short time every section of the Frontera was penetrated as increasing numbers of colonists laid claim to the unreserved portions of the area.

In this way the Araucanians, soon after their pacification in 1884, came to be confronted with a major problem of cultural readjustment. Whereas they had once been accustomed to wide stretches of free land, they were now hemmed in on fixed reservations; where they had developed a way of life that was successfully adapted to the conduct of long-drawn out wars, they were now forced to modify their customs to suit the conditions of lasting peace. It is the study of this aspect of cultural dynamics that provides one of the central themes of the present monograph.

[8] Housse, 1939, p. 282. This move may well have been influenced by the need of finding new economic outlets for veterans who were returning from four years of service in the army.

[9] McBride, 1936, p. 296.

THE ALLOTMENT PROGRAM, SINCE 1917

Unfortunately, from the viewpoint of the harassed Indians, they were yet to be faced with another difficult problem of adjustment—the transition from communally to privately owned land. At the time when reservations were first created by law, a property title (*título de merced*) was issued to each chief who was the recognized head of a kinship group that lived together. It was stipulated, though, that at the request of one-eighth of its members, any reduction must be subdivided into individually-held parcels.[10] At first the natives opposed such subdivisions since the reservation grants usually included a bit of extra land for the common use of the group, but as time went on more and more pressure was exerted to have all reservation land assigned "in severalty to each individual of the kinship group, and to dispose of any remainder for white colonization."[11] An average of five to six hectares (about twelve to fifteen acres) was supposed to be allotted to each person. Where insufficient land was available, the government was expected to provide additional parcels from within its domain. Lothrop informed me that in 1930 some families near Temuco had only one hectare, and in 1937 Dugan estimated that between Quepe and Toltén the average Indian had only two and one-half hectares.[12] According to Lothrop, some poor families in 1930 were moving up the Andes and clearing the forests to make new farms, while others were living with relatives.

Despite the existence of a protective clause that forbade Indian owners to dispose of their parcels of land for a period of ten years, native leaders were not slow to realize how completely the new system of personal land ownership would break up what was left of their tribal unity. In 1930 they held a large congress in Boroa, at which they thoroughly discussed the problems that confronted them.[13] In the end they bowed to what ap-

[10] *Ibid.*, p. 312.

[11] *Ibid.*, p. 311.

[12] Dugan, 1937, p. 13.

[13] Dr. Lothrop told of a congress that was held on Wednesday, December 25, 1929. Although it was a rainy day about four thousand people were

peared inevitable and reluctantly admitted that the continued partitioning of their lands could not be stopped. Somewhat pathetically, these descendants of the great warriors of old asked only that the government should give them adequate legal protection. Dr. McBride, who was present at the congress, was moved to express himself in a vein of gloomy prophecy. "The abolition of their agrarian communities," he wrote, "is an important event in the history of Chile, representing the virtual extinction of the long-maintained Araucanian independence."[14]

There will be occasion to study some of the details of this process hereinafter.

present, with perhaps one thousand men on horseback forming a great circle during the speeches. The immediate cause of this congress was the dislodgement of Mapuches close to Temuco so that an airport could be built. Compensation was one hundred pesos, then amounting to $12.19.

[14] McBride, 1936, p. 313.

LAND USE AND MATERIAL CULTURE

PRACTICALLY the entire length of the Frontera lies between 37 and 40 degrees, south latitude. Within this zone summers are usually dusty and hot, and winters are characterized by excessive rainfalls that turn fields into bogs and roads into successions of mudholes (Pl. V, Fig. 1). Except in the mountains, very little snow falls, and temperatures seldom go below freezing; yet the air is so damp and chill that even one accustomed to the snow and ice of winter in the northern middle latitudes finds himself cold and uncomfortable. According to McBride, most of the Frontera averages over eighty inches of rain annually, and nearly all precipitation occurs from May to September.[1] The rainy season begins late in May, reaches a climax during July and August, and tapers off in September. Each year, so local inhabitants like to tell, the drabness of winter is broken by days of warm, sunny weather that is popularly known as "the little summer of Saint John" because it is supposed to come at the time of Saint John's Day on June 24. In 1948, true enough, such a pleasant interlude did occur, except that it started about a week before the winter solstice. For the poorer groups of Indians and Chileans alike, the mid-winter months from June to August constitute a blue period because the preceding year's food is likely to be exhausted before the new crops are ready to be harvested.

There is a great deal of natural vegetation in the territory of the Mapuche. "The dense temperate rain forest begins rather abruptly at the Bío Bío and extends with only local breaks throughout the area. . . . Typical trees are deciduous and evergreen beeches . . . and cypress. . . . Of particular cultural importance are the alerce (*Fitzroya patagonica*) and canelo (*Drimys winteri*)."[2] The Chilean pine (*Araucaria imbricata*) is also common to the area and extends well up the slopes of the Andes. Some of the native groups living here are known to have used *Araucaria* piñons as a staple plant food.

[1] McBride, 1936, p. 21, Fig. 7, *et passim*.

[2] Cooper, 1946, pp. 687–88.

If one can accept the accuracy of a letter of Pedro de Valdivia, which contains what is probably the first "description of the Araucanians ever penned,"[3] the Indians were already good husbandmen in the mid-sixteenth century. Valdivia referred to their rich flocks, "with wool that drags along the ground," and to the numerous foods that they "sow for their livelihood, such as maize, potatoes, quinua [*quinoa?*], madi [*mani?*], pepper, and beans. . ."[4]

Even in the days when they were almost incessantly at war with Spaniards or Chileans, the Araucanians derived much of their sustenance from the soil. Their homeland afforded a few game animals and a number of wild fowl, but they lived primarily on a vegetarian diet. They ate many wild plants, tubers, nuts, and fruits, but they also raised crops of corn, wheat, and potatoes, together with garden products, such as peppers and onions.[5] Farming was left almost entirely to women, and intensive agriculture was seldom attempted. Land was cleared and utilized as occasion demanded, but there was no effort to improve the soil and no great concern over the exact locations and limits of land holdings.

LAND OWNERSHIP

In the Spanish period small units of kindred, whose precise composition is unknown, claimed rights of possession to the areas they occupied. Apparently, the head of a putative kin group held some sort of title on behalf of the entire unit and assigned particular plots for the use of his followers. Ownership applied only to usufruct, for it seems to have been the rule that land itself could neither be sold nor alienated. According to McBride: "It is even doubtful if any fixed practice of inheriting individual holdings had become established, though probably a family remained in possession as long as it desired."[6]

[3] Graham, 1927, p. 100.

[4] *Ibid.* It must be remembered that Valdivia sometimes exaggerated Chile's resources in order to attract followers.

[5] For further information on these topics, consult Latcham, 1909, pp. 340–41; Guevara, 1929, II: 288–330; and Moesbach, 1930, pp. 74–122.

[6] McBride, 1936, p. 309.

This lax system of land ownership and use was perfectly feasible before the reservation era because Araucanía contained more than enough space for all its inhabitants, the soil was fertile and well watered, and there was a great abundance of natural foods. A bewildering situation developed when, after 1866, the Mapuche were forced to bring their traditional practices into conformity with Chilean law. So-called chiefs found it impossible to prove their legal rights to ownership and authority over land, and ordinary tribesmen could not validate their claims to the particular plots that they customarily cultivated. When the government officials who were charged with the responsibility of marking off reservations found themselves faced with one perplexing problem after another, they were forced to adopt a technique of assigning titles more or less arbitrarily. In each instance they made inquiries to determine the individual who seemed to be the leader or headman of a local group and the extent of his domain. They then gave the tract a number and sometimes a name, marked off official boundary lines, and issued a map of the holdings together with a *título de merced*, to the supposed chief (see Fig. 5). In this way a great number of collective land holdings, known as reserves or reductions, came to be established throughout the Frontera after 1866; and one can imagine that a man occasionally found himself unexpectedly elevated to the position of cacique.[7] This situation could hardly have been avoided. No one knows what was the exact nature of chieftainship among the early historic Araucanians, and it is not improbable that some groups of natives could not tell who was chief among them. In certain cases, too, informants intimate that sly commoners took advantage of the confused situation to represent themselves as chiefs in order to acquire titles to land (see Fig. 7).

New difficulties, in addition to those inherent in the state of affairs just described, arose when the time came to subdivide the reductions in order to allot land in severalty. Foremost of these was the perplexing fact that few individuals had distinc-

[7] It should be noted that the Mapuche word for headman is *loñko,* and that the term "cacique" is a Spanish introduction.

tive names. According to Mapuche custom only surnames were used, and these were generally shared by several members of a kin group. Realizing what a puzzle it would make if they allotted titles to numerous Antipans and Huenchuals without further identification, government workers urged the Indians to adopt more distinctive names, whereupon the Araucanians promptly took such appellations as struck their fancy. Many assumed the names of the surveyors and officials who were working among them, some added Spanish given names to their native names, and others simply invented appellations at random.

As has been the case in other areas of the world, the allotment system in Chile did not work out smoothly with the passage of time. No matter how adequate and equable the original grants may have been, serious inequalities arose through the operation of inheritance customs and increase of population. For example, when the reduction of Cautinche was originally established in 1889, it consisted of 276 hectares, designed for the use of forty-four persons. In 1948, 111 people were living on the original tract.

Sometimes, too, a man found himself heir to several small parcels of land scattered over a number of reservations, no one of them large enough to sustain his family. The usual custom in such cases was to sell the odd bits for cash, and to go on a spree while the money lasted. Owners of private estates in the vicinity of Indian reductions are generally on the lookout to extend their holdings by buying up small pieces of property as they become available.[8]

The practice of granting titles in severalty also became a source of trouble because, in spite of protective clauses, it enabled individual natives to sell their property to land sharks or liquor dealers. Men who became landless generally sought work in cities, moved to Argentina to become shepherds, or hired themselves out as laborers to more fortunate tribesmen or to

[8] From time to time natives complain that, in addition to legitimate purchases, some unscrupulous landlords make a practice of moving their fences across legal boundaries in order to encompass Indian land.

the owners of the big estates known as *fundos*.[9] Some Chilean landowners employ Araucanians by preference because they are willing to work long hours for small pay, will accept poorer food and housing than Chilean workmen demand, and do not often join organized labor movements.

All in all, it can be seen that land ownership has become one of the most vexing problems confronting the Mapuche. It is aggravated by the fact that the soil which was once heavily wooded has been swept bare of its forest cover as more and more trees have been cut down to clear ground for farming, for fuel, and to provide material for houses.[10] Furthermore, the increase of livestock since pacification has led to serious overgrazing, with the result that the heavy rains of winter wash valuable chemicals out of the denuded earth and erode great tracts of precious soil as the waters cut deeply into the bare ground. In addition, the Indians have been cultivating their land much more intensively since the beginning of the reservation period than they ever had done before, without adequate programs of fertilization, crop rotation, or fallowing. It is by no means uncommon to find a native struggling year in and year out to raise two crops of wheat annually on the same piece of ground. It is no wonder that in some cases the soil has become depleted to the point where the returns are scarcely worth the effort of farming.

LAND USE

Several basic changes in land use have taken place in the last few decades. Above all, agriculture has become a major occupation for men,[11] and its practice has become intensive rather than desultory. Wheat is the principal crop, both for food and

[9] Once in a while an ambitious Araucanian who has grown sons will work for a Chilean landlord as a *mediador*, on a profit-sharing basis, while his children operate his own farm. Such men soon become far wealthier than their neighbors.

[10] Under missionary influence a few Mapuche are compensating for the loss of forest cover by planting groves of eucalyptus or apple trees on their property (Frontispiece).

[11] Women still help during planting and harvesting times, and I have observed women, in families where adult males are lacking, performing such heavy tasks as plowing.

for money, and comparatively little corn is grown. Plowing, harrowing, and similar tasks are done with conventional Spanish-Chilean tools, and the pattern of successive farming operations is the same throughout the countryside. Oxen are the favorite draught animals, and horses are rarely used for agricultural tasks.

The ideal system of land utilization throughout this part of Chile calls for a rotation of fields, whereby each plot can be left fallow after several years of use. When agricultural activities commence in the spring, preliminary plowing takes place if the soil is moist, but if the land is dry it is broken up with the aid of a toothed harrow. Before planting, a field is subjected to two more plowings, at right angles to each other, after which it is smoothed over with an improvised sort of drag, made by affixing tree branches to a harrow (Pl. I, Fig.2). Guide lines are then cut across the field at intervals of about ten feet, and as each section is seeded, it is lightly covered with soil. It must be understood, of course, that few Araucanians and not all Chileans take the trouble, or have the resources, to follow the ideal pattern.

Every Mapuche strives to sow at least six hectares of wheat. Thereafter, the principal crops consist of barley, oats, beans, peas, and potatoes. Onions, leeks, and chili peppers are grown in garden plots, most often by women, for use as condiments. Wild strawberries and other fruits are picked where available, and apple orchards are being planted in increasing numbers. Many families augment their food supplies by raising chickens and pigs; and a few enterprising souls keep turkeys, ducks, and geese. The average householder also has a yoke of work oxen, two or three all-purpose horses, and several dogs. Except for those who are destitute, each family maintains a small flock of about two dozen sheep. Excess lambs are generally sold for cash. Sheep are sheared in the spring, and the wool is spun and woven into rugs or garments by women.

A provident farmer plans to divide his yield into three parts. One is for the use of his family, a second is put aside for seed, and the third is used for paying debts or for cash sale.[12]

[12] In good years a farm will return as much as ten units of produce for every unit of seed sown. In bad years the proportion may fall as low as three

Native informants frequently bewail their poverty, and often lay much of the blame on Chilean townspeople. The following account, based on the commercial relations of Cautinche reduction with Cholchol, may be regarded as typical.

Cautinche is linked to Cholchol, which is ten kilometers distant in a straight line, by an ungraded dirt road. There are a number of small merchants in Cholchol, storekeepers, millers, liquor dealers, and others, who trade primarily with Indians. They buy farm produce and sell whatever merchandise the natives care to purchase. On occasions when a Mapuche's crops have failed he may get caught in an economic cycle which he does not understand and which usually reduces him to hopeless poverty. The reader should not forget that these statements were obtained from native residents of Cautinche, who tend to minimize their own faults and to emphasize the failings of the Chilean tradesmen. Nevertheless, there is probably much truth in their story.

When a farmer finds himself without sufficient seed for planting a new crop, he may borrow what he requires at 100 per cent interest, due at the next harvest. The Araucanians complain that although the merchants often lend poor seed that matures badly or produces numerous weeds, they always insist on being repaid with selected, high-grade seed.

Another source of trouble is the custom locally known as *cosechas en verde*, which signifies buying a green harvest. This refers to the practice of business men who send agents into the countryside each summer to buy up stands of growing crops or animals yet unborn. When an Indian enters into such a transaction he generally spends in a short time whatever cash he receives. By winter he finds that he has neither money nor food left for his family, and when spring comes he is forced to borrow seed in order to start a new crop.

There is also a standing complaint that in Cholchol practically every dealer keeps liquor on hand. When Araucanians

---

to one, a yield that is hardly worth the effort of harvesting. Cooper (1946, pp. 699–706) provided a good summary of subsistence activities. See also Latcham, 1909, pp. 343–44; and Moesbach, 1930, pp. 29–32 and 138–68.

come to town to mill their grain or to sell their surplus crops, they are encouraged to drink, with the result that they often squander their profits and return home empty-handed or with pitifully small amounts of cash.

HOUSE TYPES

For the most part the Mapuche continue to live in their traditional type of dwellings, which they call *rukas*. House building is always done in fall and winter, with the help of relatives or neighbors. If the necessary materials have been properly prepared in advance, construction can be completed in a day or two.[13] The *rukas* are generally oval or rectangular in ground plan, and average about 15 feet wide, 25 to 30 feet long, and 8 to 10 feet high. Dimensions and shapes may vary considerably from house to house, even on the same reservation. Houses are most frequently oriented in an east-west direction, with a single doorway facing east, but sometimes they are placed in other directions for greater protection from prevailing winds.

The framework of a *ruka* consists of heavy posts, set about two to three feet apart and interlaced with thin poles or canes, over which are placed tightly fitting and overlapping bundles of thatch (Pl. II, Fig. 1). There are no windows, but openings that serve as smoke holes are left at opposite ends of the roof (see Frontispiece). The floor is of firmly packed earth, near the center of which a small excavation ringed with stones is made for use as a fireplace.

Ruka interiors frequently acquire a deep brown glaze, said to result from the action of smoke. Roof beams and posts also serve for holding spare garments and tools; cooking vessels and water jars are generally left on the ground near the fireplace. Beds and bedding are ranged along the side walls.[14] Personally, I saw no *ruka* that comprised more than a single, undivided room, but Domingo Carilaf affirmed that in "better"

[13] Many additional data on house construction may be found in Guevara, 1911, p. 143; Moesbach, 1930, pp. 169–83; and Joseph, 1931*a*, pp. 12–29.

[14] For further details see Housse, 1939, pp. 158 ff.

homes a partition was used to separate the "kitchen" from the living quarters.

Despite uniformity of construction and furnishings, there are striking differences in tidiness from house to house. Some women keep their floors more evenly packed and more neatly swept than do others, and occupants vary in the amount of care with which they exclude dogs, chickens, pigs, and other animals. In a few instances large animals such as horses or oxen are sheltered indoors during inclement weather, with consequences that can easily be imagined.

Religious rites no longer accompany the occupancy of a new house, but the owner customarily provides food and drink for an all-night celebration for his helpers and friends. A literal housewarming takes place on these occasions, as extra fires are lighted on the floor.[15] It is thought that heated air rising from within, with the downward pressure of cold air outside, will make the thatch roof fit more tightly. A family may even postpone moving into a new *ruka* until the first rainy day in order to be sure that conditions are right for making it snug and weatherproof.

On none of the reductions that I visited in 1948 did I notice houses with more than one doorway, or with separate compartments for the use of a man's wives or married sons.[16] Structures with zinc, tin, or even tile roofs may be seen from time to time, but these are more likely to be storerooms or barns than habitations, as the Mapuche claim that conventional *rukas* are more comfortable. Nevertheless, one innovation has become widespread. Many dwellings are built with plank walls to a height of three to four feet and are thatched the rest of the way. As a rule, owners still build their own houses with the help of volunteers, but here and there I was shown an exceptional structure that had been built by hired carpenters from a near-by town. Often when a new *ruka* is put up the old one is converted into a barn for the use of livestock.

[15] Cf. Housse, 1939, pp. 155 ff.

[16] Arrangements of this sort are frequently mentioned. See, for example, Smith, 1855, pp. 295–96; and Housse, 1939, pp. 157–59.

Within the traditional homes the central fireplace provides the only artificial light and heat that the occupants enjoy, although candles and kerosene lamps are gradually being adopted by those who can afford them. Cooking is done at the open fire, often in pots that are suspended by chains. Pottery vessels were formerly the rule, but commercially made iron utensils are now common. Wood is the chief fuel, but straw may be used to build up a refractory fire. Unlike farmers in the United States, who take pride in having neat and ample piles of seasoned wood, the Araucanians have the custom of dragging several large pieces of timber into their yards. Here the wood lies exposed to the weather and, whenever necessary, someone hurries outdoors and chops off a few sticks. Even in the rainy season no attempt is made to store up a large quantity of dry wood. At night, fires are neither extinguished nor kept going. They are generally covered and left smouldering so that they may readily be blown up the next day.

SETTLEMENT PATTERN

One of the most striking aspects of a contemporary Araucanian reservation is the absence of any formal distribution of houses: "There are no streets, no central plaza, no stores or public buildings, in short, nothing that suggests the spatial arrangement of a village or town."[17] Not infrequently, houses are built in small clusters of three or four, known as *lofche*, but single dwellings that stand apart are common. As a general rule, each home is within view of several others, but rarely do footpaths connect the structures. This separation has been noted by a number of writers, but it has never been completely explained.

Very likely, the antipathy of the Mapuche for spatial cohesion may originally have been a reflection of their loosely knit social organization, and it may also have been an expression of their deep desire for independence. Then again, during the era of steady fighting such a settlement pattern may doubtless have had strategic significance, for no enemy commander was likely

[17] Titiev, 1949, p. 3.

to organize large-scale expeditions in order to attack a handful of widely scattered residences. Still, too much separation would have rendered each isolated homestead particularly vulnerable. By way of compromise a system seems to have been worked out whereby houses were erected within sight of one another. This meant that by day smoke signals could be used for summoning help in the event of a raid. The same proximity also gave assurance that at night the sound of the *kullkull* could be heard. A *kullkull* is a simple wind instrument fashioned from a cow horn and used like an army bugle. In case of danger a signal was blown, consisting of two long, two short, and a very long blast. When this was heard men rushed to the nearest road to intercept or attack any raiders. It is not improbable that the scarcity of roads on the reservations also resulted from strategic considerations, as it enabled local defenders to concentrate on a limited number of points.

At the present time the settlement pattern seems to reflect little more than cultural conservatism, combined with the desire of each householder to live in private on his own particular piece of property. The privacy of each residence is greatly respected. Conventionally, no one ever enters the home of another person without an express invitation. Inmates of a house are made aware of a visitor by the barking of their dogs who rush fiercely at a stranger; sometimes a child appears at the door to discover who has come. From a safe distance the caller shouts, "*Mari, mari, papai!*" ("A hundred [greetings] little grandmother!"), or a similar phrase. If the occupants so desire they respond and invite the visitor to come in, but if there is no reply the visitor is expected to go away even if he is aware that someone is home.

The modern Mapuche are not much given to long distance travel. Short journeys may be made afoot, but men, in particular, prefer to ride horseback on longer trips, and they are very much at ease in the saddle. When women have to travel for a considerable distance they generally ride in an oxcart, with a masculine relative or companion as driver. As was previously stated, roads are virtually nonexistent inside a given reservation, and those leading to the Chilean towns or from one reduction to another are little more than wagon trails, unsurfaced, ungraded, and rarely kept in repair. Ordinarily, they can be used by oxcart except in the rainy season, when they are passable, if at all, only on horseback (Pl. V, Fig. 1).

One of the factors that has served to augment the isolation of Mapuche reservations is the increase of fences. This is particularly noteworthy in the case of large *fundos,* which are likely to be completely enclosed, thus forcing travelers to make long detours.

Throughout the area the hardships of winter travel are most clearly manifested in cases of severe illness. Our attention was called to numerous instances of people from Cholchol who, when stricken with appendicitis, had to travel several hours on horseback to reach a hospital. We also witnessed a very dramatic event on the night of July 5, 1948, when an Araucanian young woman attempted suicide by shooting herself in the stomach. About a dozen men took turns in wretched weather to carry her twenty miles in an improvised litter to the mission hospital in Cholchol. She was given first aid and ordered to go to Nueva Imperial for further treatment. This necessitated another long journey over miserable roads in a small cart. We were unable to learn whether or not the patient survived the trip, for a storm blew down Cholchol's telephone connections.

FOOD HABITS

The preparation of food is a principal concern of the women. Wheat is the main staple; most commonly it is ground to flour and parched or toasted to make *mürke.* It is then usually stirred into hot or cold water to form a gruel or porridge that is called *chaikan* if salted, and *wilpud* or *ullpud* if sweetened. Wheat flour is also mixed with water, salt, and leavening to prepare a dough that is baked in hot ashes to make a tortilla-like bread called *remulkofke.* Occasionally, too, bread dough is fried in deep fat, in the form of a large circular roll (*iwinkofke*) that has a crisp crust and a soft interior.

Apparently, the Araucanians do not adhere strictly to the

pattern of eating three times a day at fixed intervals, nor do they have names for their meals. When one informant was purposely pressed into designating the meals by names, he gave the following terms: breakfast, *liwen korü* ("early morning soup"); lunch, *raniañtu korü* ("noonday soup"); and supper, *pun·korü* ("night soup").[18]

There is not a great deal of variety to the customary diet. Soup or gruel is the main dish, eaten with bread whenever there is any. Breakfast is taken between sunrise and eight in the morning. It usually consists of coarsely ground, unparched wheat, mixed with water, and flavored with salt and greens such as *yuyo*,[19] young leeks or scallions, chili peppers, and coriander. This standard soup, to which lard may be added when available, is called *tikin korü*. Sometimes, *chaikan* or *ullpud* is eaten instead, and on occasion a change is provided in the form of an oatmeal or bran soup, *chikal korü*, enriched and flavored in the usual way.[20]

If a man departs very early for work, he may do without his breakfast or arrange to have soup and bread sent out to him.

The midday meal is ordinarily eaten in the *ruka* between noon and three. Most often it consists of bread and a sort of succotash, *pisku*, made by cooking together beans, peas, corn, potatoes, and greens.[21] Occasionally, yerba maté is drunk at this time.

Supper is eaten well after sundown, and is much like breakfast except that those who have it drink yerba maté at night.

[18] Moesbach (1930, p. 191) reported that formerly only two meals were eaten daily. The only term for a particular meal listed by Augusta (1916, I: 65) is *iaqel*, for which he gave *comida* as a translation. *Comida* may mean any meal, but more commonly it is used for supper or dinner in the evening. Latcham (1909, p. 342) said that there are no special names for their meals.

[19] *Yuyo* refers to vegetables of the mustard-turnip group (*Brassica*). Additional details regarding Araucanian food usages may be found in Molina (1808, II: 105 ff.) and in Latcham (1909, pp. 340–43).

[20] Cornmeal was sometimes put in for thickening. When available, macaroni or spaghetti is now added.

[21] I was told by Mrs. Donaldson that both Indian and Chilean women usually throw away "the first water," i.e., the vitamin-rich water in which the vegetables are cooked.

Yerba maté may also be taken by groups of men as a sort of afternoon tea on festive occasions. A host's womenfolk prepare and hand to him a cup nearly filled with dry leaves, and a small tea kettle of boiling water. The host fills the cup with hot water and offers it to a guest who sips the free liquid through a narrow hollow tube (bombilla), commonly fashioned from brass. Then the cup is refilled with hot water and goes the rounds until everyone has had enough. Because the tea leaves absorb most of the fluid, a man can drink six or eight cups without getting a great deal of liquid.

In the region under discussion fish is unavailable, and meat is seldom eaten, except during fiestas. The roasted flesh of sheep, cows, pigs, chickens, and other poultry is much enjoyed, but the favorite meat is that of a young mare. When meat is included in the daily diet, it is most often made part of the midday meal.

Several traditional beverages continue to be consumed in large amounts. Fruit, cereal, and vegetable extracts, mixed with water and usually fermented, are old-time favorites. Most popular of all are: *chicha*, a cider made from the juice of mashed apples;[22] *mote*, made of decorticated wheat or corn boiled in water;[23] *mudai*, prepared from wheat with the skin on;[24] and *muska* or *chicha de maiz*, a fermented beverage prepared with premasticated corn.[25] All of these drinks are commonly allowed to develop an alcoholic content, and early chroniclers are agreed that the Araucanians have long been addicted to intoxicants, particularly at fiestas.[26] Some nineteenth-century observers have pointed out that the incidence of drunkenness increased rapidly in the reservation period, for every Chilean town in the

[22] Latcham (1909, p. 343) reported that apple *chicha* is made by men. Other fruits are sometimes substituted for apples. The presence of pips in a drink used to be considered an omen of fertility.

[23] Skin was removed with a strong solution of ashes. Cf. Joseph, 1931*a*, p. 92.

[24] Good accounts of *mudai* manufacture may be found in Moesbach, 1930, pp. 145–46, and in Housse, 1939, pp. 172–75.

[25] Augusta, 1934, p. 13. A vivid reaction to the premastication process occurs in Smith, 1885, pp. 302–4.

[26] Cooper, 1946, p. 741.

Frontera became a center for the sale of cheap but powerful liquor.[27] Unscrupulous tradesmen, as has already been mentioned, regularly encourage the Indians to drink when a transaction is being made, and alcoholism is currently a major problem.[28]

At meals women used to serve adult men first and children after their elders, but it has become the practice for family groups to eat together. Home made wooden bowls, platters, ladles, and spoons were formerly widely employed,[29] but store-bought enamel cups, metal pots and tea kettles, inexpensive "china," and tin spoons are now coming into use.

The only universal food tabus apply to snakes and frogs. In addition, young people are forbidden to eat sheep testicles, lest girls develop pains in the breasts and boys suffer from aching testes. Growing children are not allowed to eat bone marrow, because it is regarded as a "watery" substance that will retard their development. Furthermore, to ensure that they will not engage in premature sexual activity, adolescent girls may not eat unripe fruit, and grown women must abstain from fish lest, like them, they refuse to settle into permanent homes.[30]

Tobacco smoking, particularly in pipes, is reported to have been widespread among elderly people, especially men.[31] The absence of native tobacco, and the expense of standard brands have combined to eliminate this custom on most reservations. Such smoking as I personally observed was done by young men who occasionally accepted the offer of a cigarette.

[27] Natives most often drink a cheap wine nowadays, fortified by the addition of strong roots, herbs, or nut shells. One big drink often intoxicates them, sometimes to the point of stupefaction. Some manage to ride home, but others fall by the roadside to sleep off the effects.

[28] Latcham (1909, p. 335) expressed himself strongly on this point.

[29] For the manufacture of a wide variety of wooden utensils, see Joseph, 1931*a*, pp. 53–85.

[30] The details of food tabus were obtained only from a single informant, J. M. Collío. These data need to be checked before they can be regarded as widespread Araucanian beliefs. Some comparative material is given in Guevara, 1929, II: 163–66.

[31] Guevara, 1911, pp. 253–82. Stone pipes occur abundantly in archaeological deposits.

DRESS

Araucanian males of all ages have abandoned their old-style costumes almost entirely, except for the constant wearing of woolen ponchos (Spanish, *manta*; Mapuche, *makuñ*). The most common garb for all occasions consists of a pair of woolen trousers, usually threadbare or repeatedly patched, an inexpensive cotton shirt, a short poncho that covers the chest and back, and a felt hat (Pl. IX, Fig. 2). When no hat is used, men generally bind a colored handkerchief about the forehead. Shoes are sometimes worn, and oxhide sandals may be utilized in winter, but most often men go barefooted. Chaps or trousers of untanned rawhide are occasionally worn by men when they must travel over muddy roads, and two or three ponchos are put on, one above another, on cold days. Except for differences of size, little boys dress in the same fashion as do adults (Frontispiece).

Young women usually wear simple cotton house dresses, aprons, shoes, stockings, and if they can be obtained, such conventional undergarments as slips or chemises. By way of contrast, older women generally wear more traditional styles of clothing. Their most essential garment still consists of the untailored type of heavy woolen dress that is called a *chamal*. It is draped over the left shoulder, where it is fastened with a pin, frequently nowadays with a huge safety pin, and it is passed under the right armpit so that it envelops the body and hangs almost to the ankles.[32] It is held at the waist with a woven sash or belt that encircles the figure twice and is looped at the left side. An apron is commonly worn over the *chamal*, and when the weather is cool a shawl is draped over the shoulders and may be fastened in front with a large safety pin. A kerchief or scarf is the conventional head covering and is usually the brightest part of the daily costume. Some of the older women wear shoes, but most of them go barefoot; and in general they do not wear stockings or undergarments.

[32] The cut of the *chamal* leaves the left shoulder bare. At present, a blouse is worn under the traditional garment. Further information on the subject of clothing may be obtained in Latcham, 1909, p. 336; Lothrop, 1930, pp. 326–29; and Moesbach, 1930, pp. 209–11.

On festive days, or when going into town in the summer months, women of all ages like to wear old-fashioned dress and ornaments. In addition to the blouse, *chamal*, belt, apron, and shawl, they put narrow bands of colored silk ribbon across the head from front to back. These strips of ribbon take the place of a kerchief and are held in position by a band of metal disks, known as a *trarüloñko*, that encircles the head above the ears (Pl. IV, Fig. 2). The hair is worn at the back in two long braids, between which a single bright ribbon may be tied to form a sort of *H*. Earrings are much in favor, and against the breast is worn a large pendant called a *trapelakucha*. Both the *trarüloñko* and the *trapelakucha* used to be fashioned of silver, and women who own such heirlooms wear them proudly. Recently, however, these ornaments have been made of baser metals such as nickel.

ARTS AND CRAFTS

In no regard is the transitional character of Araucanian culture more notable than in the field of native technology. Until recent times the Mapuche practiced a wide range of arts and crafts, but today the only activity of the sort that survives everywhere is the spinning of wool and weaving on hand looms. Nearly all women learn to spin and weave. In their spare time they make many things for home use and can always find a market in town for the surplus. From numerous references in the literature one gathers that Araucanian craftsmen formerly manufactured many objects of stone and wood, and that many of them were fine basketmakers, potters, and silversmiths.[33] At present, a specialist here and there continues one or another of the traditional crafts,[34] and the others purchase what they want

[33] A large body of literature is devoted to Araucanian arts and crafts. Many references may be found in Cooper, 1946, pp. 713–19; and in Brand, 1941*a*, pp. 29–33. Good studies of stone and wood work, basketry, and pottery are available in Joseph, 1931*a*. For weaving, see Lothrop, 1930; Joseph, 1931*b*; and Oyarzún and Latcham, 1928. Silver work is described in Fontecilla, 1946. Guevara (1929, II: 247–85) provided a general treatment of native industries.

[34] At Cautinche, for example, even the custom of weaving has almost gone out of existence. A number of women still weave at Carrarriñe and

directly from him or in the adjacent cities, where there are usually shops specializing in native wares.

Although the making of new musical instruments is currently much curtailed, many traditional implements are still used. Commonest of all is the *pifullka*, which ranges from a small hollow tube of cane, bamboo, or reed that is blown like a simple whistle to a rudimentary kind of bitonal Pan pipe fashioned from laurel wood. The latter is the older style and consists of a hollow chamber, divided into two parts by a wooden septum. The newer kinds of *pifullkas* may be blown on any occasion, but the old-fashioned instrument is reserved for ceremonial events. It is blown in conjunction with dancing, its higher note signifying fast time, and the lower one a slower tempo.

Another common wind instrument is the *trutruka* (Pl. XI, Fig. 1), which consists of a section of hollow cane or bamboo, about eight to ten feet long, to one end of which a cow horn is attached. Before it is used it is cleared by dipping water into the cow horn and letting it run out at the opposite end, which serves as the mouthpiece. *Trutrukas* are in evidence on all important occasions, particularly at assemblies such as *ñillatuns* and funerals. One specimen, owned by Pedro Llancao, husband of Cautinche's medicine woman, was fashioned from a length of hollow metal pipe affixed to a cow horn. When blown it gave forth a series of notes approximating G, C, G, E, C, two octaves below middle C. All *trutrukas* have only a limited range and are played a few notes at a time with lengthy intervals of rest. The sounds are mournful and not very melodic by our standards.

A third wind instrument is called a *llollkin*. It is much less common than the *trutruka* and is employed primarily at funerals. It is considerably shorter than a *trutruka* and is played by taking in the breath. A *llollkin* is made from about two to three feet of hollow cane or bamboo, attached to a cow horn, and is cleared like a *trutruka*, with water (Pl. IX, Fig. 2). It has a greater melodic range and is pleasing to the Western ear, even

Renaco, but in no one of these places is there a single specialist in woodworking, pottery, basketry, or metallurgy.

though it is used for sad effects. Informants agree that the traditional tunes of the *llollkin* convey specific messages to native auditors.

Percussive instruments include gourd rattles, small strings of metal sleigh bells, and *kul·truñs*. The last are drums that are widely used in rituals by the shamans known as *machis*. A *kul·truñ* is made of horse or dog skin, tightly stretched over a wooden bowl-shaped frame that is neither very deep nor very wide (Pl. VIII). Generally, it contains a few pebbles or dried beans, so that at times it can serve as a kind of rattle. Before being used the *kul·truñ* is usually warmed at a fire. When played by a *machi* a *kul·truñ* is held in one hand and beaten by a single drumstick in the other. On some occasions, however, a layman may act as drummer, using a pair of slender sticks.

The skin surface of a typical *kul·truñ* is decorated by curved marks that stand for the roots of trees and other vegetation, and by parallel lines crossing at right angles to form quadrants, each of which represents a quarter of the globe (Pl. VIII). The small square at the center is known as *rañiñmapu* ("middle of the earth"). To an Araucanian everyone who does not originate from *rañiñmapu* is a stranger. Telling someone to go to *rañiñmapu* is equivalent to trying to get rid of him by sending him on a futile journey to a mythical place.

Despite the variety of musical instruments known to the Mapuche,[35] their music does not seem to be highly developed as measured by Euro-American standards.

THE ROUND OF DAILY TASKS

A degree of sexual dichotomy still prevails in the conduct of daily tasks, but it is not rigidly observed in all cases. Women, as is universally the rule, are expected to do the housekeeping, including the making of beds, sweeping and tidying up the *ruka*, preparing and serving meals, and repairing and washing clothing. They have complete charge of the care and rearing of infants, and, as has already been noted, they spend much time

[35] *Pifullkas*, *trutrukas*, and *kul·truñs* are described in Joseph, 1931*a*, pp. 72–77. The *llollkin* does not seem to have been previously reported.

weaving ponchos, blankets, belts, and dresses. Water is fetched by women, although men sometimes lend a hand, and it is not unusual for women to raise garden produce, care for flocks of poultry, and help with some phases of farming and house building.

Mapuche men are expected to do most of the heavy manual labor connected with farming, such as care for the oxen and horses, construct houses, gather fuel, and cut wood. They also make a few implements such as hockey sticks and simple flutes or whistles, and they serve as drivers whenever a journey has to be made by oxcart.

An observer from the United States is inevitably struck by the disproportionate amount of work that is done by children. In fact, a woman with grown but unmarried daughters and a man with unwed, adolescent sons may be said to live "in retirement." Such parents will, as a rule, lie abed late or remain indoors when the weather is bad, while the girls cook and look after the house and the boys attend to the outdoor chores. Regardless of weather it is a common sight to see boys as young as ten to twelve handling a yoke of oxen hitched to a plow or a cart (Pl. I, Figs. 1 and 2). It must not be thought that children are unhappy or resentful under these circumstances, for they are not. On the contrary, they are generally pleased to be treated as adults, and boys, especially, are proud and joyful to be entrusted with the responsibilities of grown-ups.

Araucanian men are frequently charged with being shiftless and lazy, and there is considerable truth to these accusations. Except at planting and harvesting times they do not exert themselves very much. One must realize, however, how few are the outlets or rewards for ambition. Those who live on reductions have little opportunity to gain money, and without money they cannot buy whatever may be necessary to better their condition. Consequently, as a group, the people tend to be apathetic, as though pervaded by a spirit of hopelessness. This applies particularly to young adults of both sexes, some of whom annually foresake the reservations in order to seek work in cities.

One cannot study the economics and material culture of the contemporary Araucanians without coming to a sharp realization of the difficulties that beset a society whose culture is in the process of undergoing a major transition. In the case of the Mapuche the change has had a much greater and more depressing effect on the men than it has had on the women. After all, the customary housekeeping and child-rearing duties of women have undergone relatively little modification and, to a large extent, the shift from war to peace has considerably lightened their agricultural labors.

This is not true for the men. Adjustment for them calls for adaptation to several drastic changes. Traditionally occupied with war and strenuous games and exercises, they must now accept the role of peaceful tillers of the soil. Inasmuch as their old culture pattern assigned no masculine prestige value to skill in agriculture, they are at best indifferent farmers. They raise what crops they can, but they take paths of least resistance instead of bending all their efforts toward the improvement of their lands, herds, and livestock. Time hangs heavy on their hands at many points of the calendar, and it is not hard to see why many of them seek to escape reality by getting drunk as often as possible.

Oddly enough, most of the Mapuches are in the habit of going to bed late and awakening fairly early, even in the rainy winter season when there is little work to be done. Again and again one hears them say: "How long the nights are!" Sometimes they beguile themselves with songs, stories, or general conversation, but even when time drags they do not like to retire early in the evening.

There is no way of predicting what cultural innovations or value systems the Araucanians may develop at a future date, but at the moment their material culture and its immediate consequences are depressingly low. Yet they are not sharply set apart from their neighbors, and except for the retention of the Mapuche language, they are virtually indistinguishable from the poorer Chilean farmers who live in their vicinity.

KINSHIP AND SOCIOPOLITICAL ORGANIZATION

Knowledge of a people's kinship system is an absolute prerequisite for an understanding of their sociopolitical organization, but such information is not easy to obtain among the Araucanians because of the transitional state of their culture. As Father Cooper wrote recently on one aspect of the subject: "There has occurred considerable change of terminology since the first decade of the 17th century."[1] The same may be said of several other kinship usages. Some of the traditional practices still persist in their entirety, others are maintained only in part, a few forms are no longer carried on but are plainly recalled, and some have disappeared altogether. Any modern description of Araucanian kinship must, accordingly, reckon with chronology. It might be possible to disregard considerations of time by presenting an account that is correct for a given moment, but such a procedure would tend to convey a false impression of a static situation, whereas the one under consideration is truly dynamic. But to give due weight to chronology by presenting a whole series of successive pictures in separate compartments is utterly impractical. By way of compromise it has been decided to place the emphasis of this report on present usages but to include those customs of former times that are vividly remembered and a knowledge of which is necessary for purposes of analysis and interpretation.

Because of the complexities involved in the study of kinship, great care was exercised to obtain reliable data. At least a dozen informants, living in various places, were utilized. In most instances complete schedules of relationship terms were obtained, and in some cases these were supplemented by the gathering of genealogical tables, together with the appropriate kinship designations applied to each relative. When the data were compared and analyzed a reasonably consonant system emerged.

[1] Cooper, 1946, p. 724. Comparative lists of kinship terms are available in many works including Latcham, 1909, pp. 357–58, 1924, pp. 344–58; Guevara, 1929, I: 333–34; and Moesbach, 1930, pp. 194–206.

KINSHIP TERMS AND PRINCIPLES OF NOMENCLATURE

From all accounts it appears most likely that the central features of Mapuche nomenclature are geared to the marriage practices. Among these, the greatest importance must be attributed to unilateral cross-cousin marriage, whereby a man is expected to marry his mother's brother's daughter. A bride goes to live with her husband in his natal household. Informants were unanimously agreed that cross-cousin mating was almost universal until approximately a generation ago. Such marriages are not at all unusual nowadays, but they are no longer as prevalent as formerly. Another important aspect is polygyny, which was once the accepted rule, but has now become the exception. This means that levirate, sororate, sororal polygyny, and wife inheritance have been almost completely given up. Nevertheless, these usages are known to have been widespread and are still reflected in the terminology.

If the kinship system is examined from the viewpoint of an adult male (Fig. 2), one finds that he calls his potential mate, the daughter of his mother's brother, *ñuke*. The same term is used to designate mother, and a derivative, *ñukentu*, is applied to mother's sister. In accordance with traditional marriage practices, a grown man might well have been wedded to all three of these persons. This would come about if *ego's* father, through the operation of the sororate or sororal polygyny, had married *ego's* mother and her sister and at death had transmitted them both to *ego* by filial inheritance. Under such circumstances it frequently was the case that a man found himself married to a cross-cousin, a mother,[2] and a mother's sister, all of whom were

[2] Little is known of Araucanian incest regulations. Latcham (1909, p. 360) and Cooper (1946, p. 719) agreed that under filial inheritance a man inherited his father's wives, except for his own mother. Yet both writers (Latcham, *op. cit.*, p. 356, and Cooper, *loc. cit.*) reported that incest of all degrees frequently occurred during drinking bouts.

Latcham (1924, p. 527) argued that the Mapuche once limited descent ties so closely to the matrilineal line that no incest tabus applied to relations between half-brothers and sisters, step-parents and step-children, and fathers and daughters.

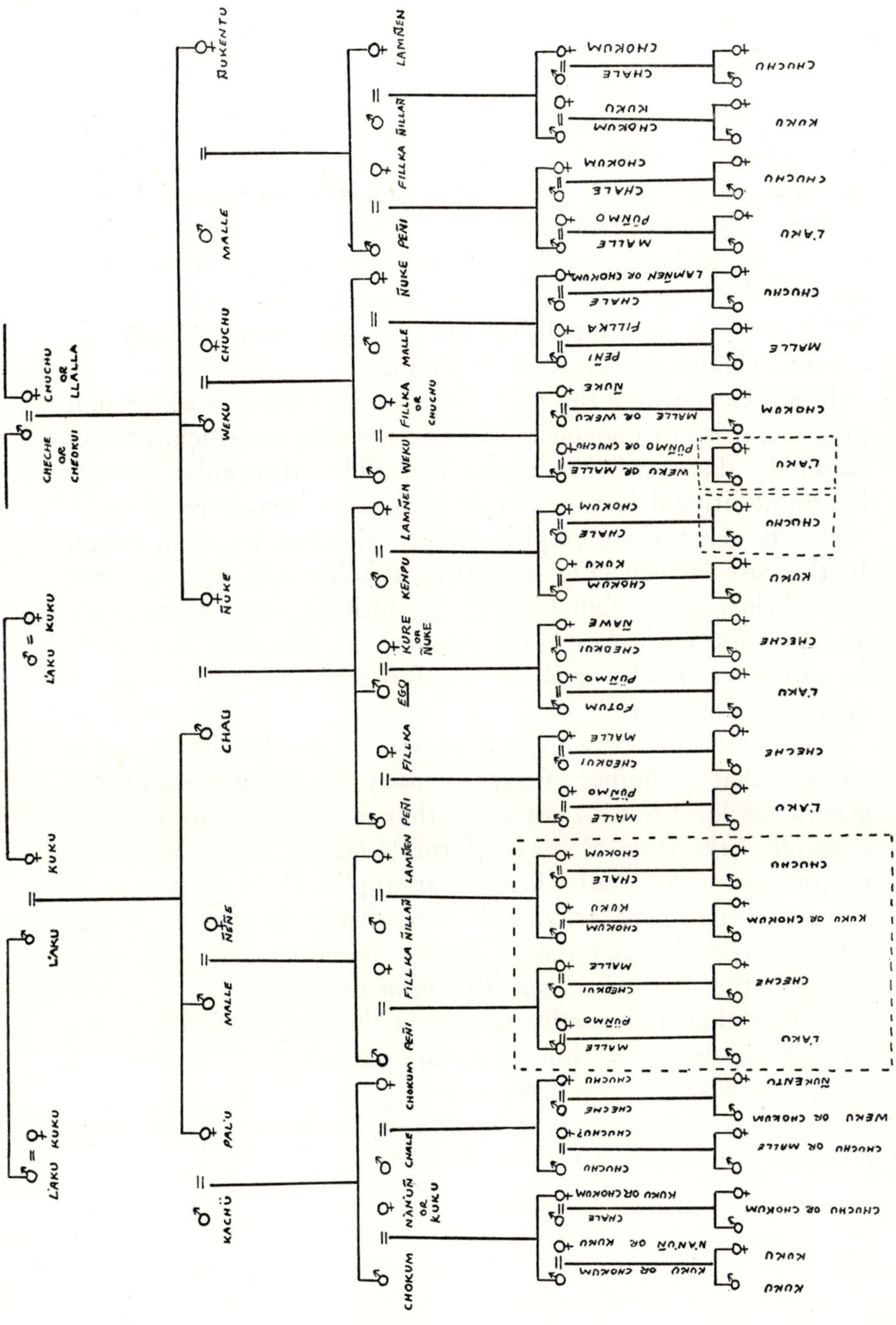

FIG. 2. The Araucanian kinship system, male speaking. For the terms inclosed by broken lines, which should be regarded as tentative, informants failed to reach close agreement.

ñuke to him. A similar tendency to use the same term for wife and mother appears in the generation above that of *ego*, since maternal uncle's wife and mother are both called *chuchu*.

Levirate and sororate were voluntarily invoked by some informants to explain other aspects of terminology. Thus, it was pointed out that *malle* conveyed the meaning of potential stepfather. Through the levirate, father's brother (*malle*) would become *ego's* father; and through the sororate, the husband of *ego's* mother's sister (*malle*) might likewise become *ego's* father. It follows logically that the offspring of these men, *ego's* parallel cousins, should be regarded as siblings.

In a society where the filial inheritance of wives is a common practice, it is not unexpected to find that the nomenclature occasionally disregards generation lines. The Araucanian system has an additional feature of this kind, since certain relatives in alternate generations employ reciprocal terms for each other. In the case of men (Fig. 2), father's father and son's son are *l·aku*. When *ego* is female (Fig. 3), father's mother and son's daughter are known as *kuku*, mother's mother and daughter's daughter are *chuchu* or *llalla*, and father's sister and brother's daughter are *pal·u*.

Another noteworthy aspect of Araucanian kinship terminology is that a number of terms convey sex distinctions at one generation level but do not serve that purpose at another. For example, *l·aku* (Fig. 2) means father's father, and *kuku* refers to father's mother; but when a man applies these terms to the grandchildren's generation there is no distinction of sex. *L· aku* refers to *ego's* brother's son's son or daughter, and *kuku* designates either *ego's* sister's son's son or daughter.

Still another noteworthy feature is the use of specific terms for certain relatives within a general category that is designated by a classificatory term. For instance, a man calls a male relative-in-law in his own generation *ñillan*, but he uses *kenpu* when referring to his own sister's husband.[3]

[3] Other examples, which are not shown because they were reported by only a single informant (J. M. Collío), are: *dea* applied by a man to his own sister, whereas *lamñen* is the classificatory term for sister or female parallel

Kinship terms are widely employed for direct address in ordinary social intercourse. Whenever a specific relationship exists between speakers, teknonymy is utilized. If there is no close relationship, terms of address[4] are used as listed in Table I.

Araucanian kinship terminology recognizes only five generations, two above and two below *ego*. If it is found necessary to extend terms to higher or lower generations, the Mapuche do not use new words, but employ numerical prefixes as needed.

TABLE I

TERMS OF DIRECT ADDRESS

Male Speaker	Person Addressed	Female Speaker
füchachau	Very old man	*chachai*
kusepapai	Very old woman	*ñaña*
chau or *chachai*	Older man than *ego*	*chau*
papai[5]	Older woman than *ego*	*papai*
peñi	Man of *ego's* age	*lamñen*
lamñen	Woman of *ego's* age	*lamñen*
fotum or *fochum*	Younger man	*welche*
lamñen	Younger woman	*paillao*
fochumtu	Very young man	*chachaiñu*
lamñentu	Very young woman	*ñañaitu*

For instance, a man calls his paternal grandfather *l·aku*. Hence, great-grandfather is *epuchi* ("twice") *l·aku*, great-

cousin; *chedkui*, used by a male to indicate his actual father-in-law, whereas *weku* applies to any one of his mother's brothers or potential fathers-in-law; and *koñi*, a term of affection used by a woman toward a favored father's sister's son, whereas other cross-cousins of this kind are generally called either *chau* ("father") or *fotum* ("son").

[4] Terms of direct address are almost invariably preceded by the Mapuche greeting, "*Mari, mari,*" which means "ten, ten," and has the connotation of a hundred greetings or welcomes.

There are so many alternate usages possible for terms of direct address that the data given in Table I require confirmation and further study.

[5] *Papai* is the most common respectful term of direct address used by either sex when speaking to an adult woman.

great-grandfather is *külachi* ("thrice") *l·aku* and so on. To take another example, a man's daughter's son is *cheche*, great-grandson is *epuchi cheche*, great-great-grandson is *külachi cheche*, and so on.[6]

Mapuche informants are most consistent and self-assured when dealing with direct patrilineal lineage connections. They are somewhat less sure of the correct terminology on the matrilineal side, particularly in the matter of collateral relationships. They are least certain when asked to give terms for collateral relatives in the two generations below *ego*. Yet, in spite of some confusion in recalling relationship designations when interviewed, people like to keep track of all their kin, and they are said to repeat family histories frequently at public gatherings or in private conversation. Whenever the great *ñillatun* ceremony is held, an occasion is provided for renewing acquaintance with one's remoter kindred. During a pause that always precedes the serving of the midday lunch all the visiting men, many of whom come from distant reductions, range themselves in a line. Thereupon, the male residents of the home reservation go down the line shaking hands and exchanging kin terms with each guest. Specific terms are used whenever the relationship of two men is clearly known, but in other cases resort is made to the general terms of direct address that are listed in Table I. Shaking hands and exchanging terms of kinship are not perfunctory. Two men will often engage in a bit of preliminary discussion before they decide on the correct terms to use. On one occasion, when I was invited to stand in the guest line, I was unhesitatingly addressed as *peñi* ("brother") by each adult host, and as *chau* ("father") by youngsters.

KINSHIP BEHAVIOR

With respect to the reciprocal behavior of kindred, as in the case of relationship terminology, the central features pertain to marriage customs. Once again, the main factor is the pattern of conduct that exists between a man and his potential mate,

[6] Cf. Latcham, 1909, p. 357.

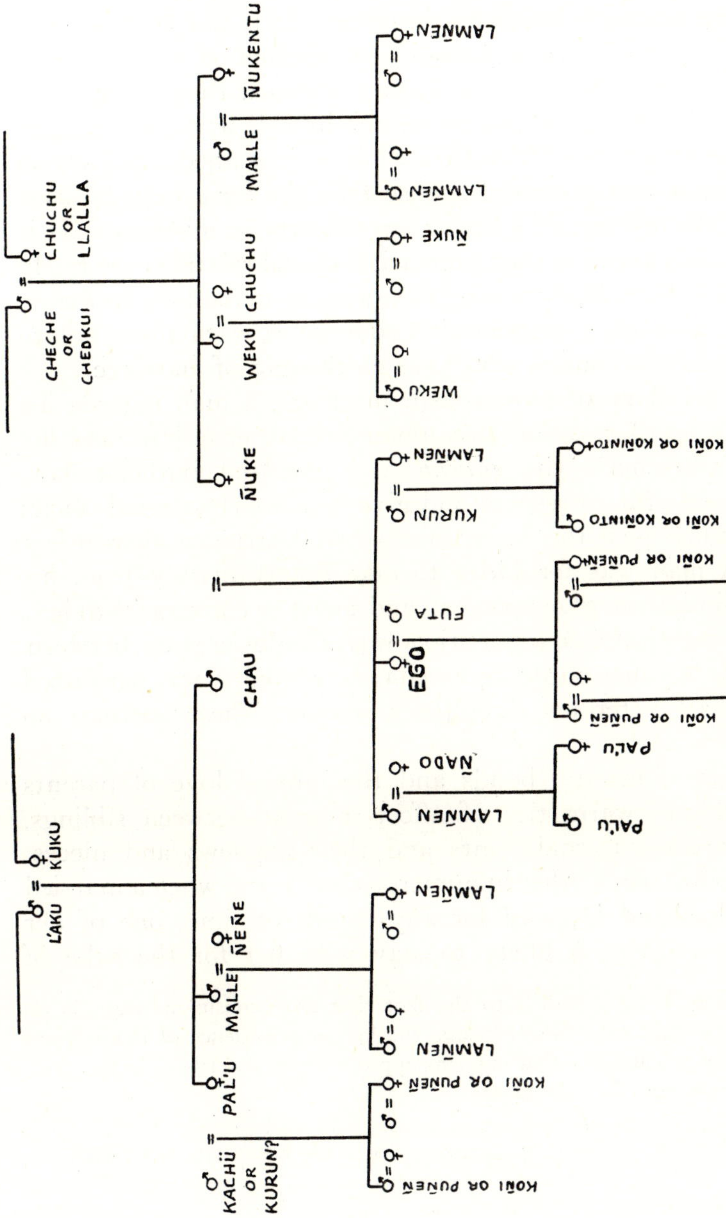

FIG. 3. The Araucanian kinship system, female speaking.

ñuke, the mother's brother's daughter.[7] It is not surprising to find that a considerable amount of freedom of intercourse is permitted to such relatives. From childhood they are encouraged to play together and to sit side by side at family gatherings, and they remain friendly for life. So ingrained is the notion that a *ñuke* is a potential spouse that the term may be used loosely for any one of a man's sweethearts or mistresses. It is by no means positive that premarital sexual relations are freely permitted. Very likely young men seek to make love to *ñukes*, but the parents of eligible girls sometimes warn them not to yield readily to cousins who have no thought of marriage.[8]

As a corollary of cross-cousin marriage, a man regards his mother's brother, *weku*, as a potential father-in-law, and his mother's brother's wife, *chuchu*, as a potential mother-in-law. A boy is taught to respect and give help to a maternal uncle; and in times past the Araucanians had a strict mother-in-law tabu. A man was forbidden to take things directly from his mother-in-law, to gaze upon her, and to eat or converse with her. If they were indoors, a partition was usually erected between them; if they met outdoors by chance, a woman was permitted only to ask after her daughter's welfare. These customs no longer prevail.[9]

Outside of marital bonds and the mutual love of parents and children, warm ties of affection exist between siblings, and between paternal aunts and their nephews and nieces. Brothers help each other in numerous ways, and when a married sister's husband is away for any length of time, one of her younger brothers is likely to stay with her for the sake of

[7] Attention is again called to the fact that cross-cousin marriage is no longer a universal rule. Nevertheless, the former prevalence of this custom is so vividly remembered that it seems appropriate to describe it in the present rather than in the past tense.

[8] Titiev, 1949, pp. 14–16.

[9] It is hard to reconcile the existence of a mother-in-law tabu with the prevalent practice of patrilocal residence. Possibly, the clearly recalled custom of mother-in-law avoidance points to an earlier rule of matrilocal residence.

company. Girls often weave ponchos for their brothers, and when a boy is in trouble he may sing a lament, pleading with a sister to help him out. At Carrarriñe we were several times visited by a younger sister of Luciano Huentacura, a widower. Whenever she was offered something special to eat she would put it aside for one of Luciano's little daughters, whom she was helping to rear. At the same time, an older sister of Luciano was bringing up one of his motherless sons in her own home.

In terms of behavior, father's brother is often equated with father, and mother's sister with mother. Aurora, wife of Juan Antinao, had been brought up by a mother's sister whom she looked upon as a parent and now, in middle age, Aurora was reciprocating by caring for one of her sister's daughters.

Much affection also prevails between paternal grandparents and grandchildren.[10] They employ reciprocal terminology, and paternal grandparents generally bestow their own names on first-born grandchildren of the appropriate sex.

It is not uncommon to find a child of poor parents living as a kind of servant in the home of a relative. Arrangements of this sort may be formed by any kinfolk, but are most commonly made by agreement between siblings. These cases involve boys more than they do girls. Such adoptive children perform all manner of chores in exchange for food, lodging, and such things as castoff clothing. They are generally expected to do little more than their more fortunate age mates and are treated much like the natal members of the household.

There is no record of institutionalized joking relationships.[11] It was said that girls joked only with their sisters, but boys were permitted to joke privately with siblings, sons of father's brothers, and brothers-in-law. Secondarily, boys joked with sisters-in-law and father's brothers. Occasionally, joking occurred between a man and the daughter of his father's brother. This topic is in need of further investigation and elucidation.

[10] In a patrilocal society a youngster would have no opportunity to enter nto intimate relations with his maternal grandparents.

[11] Cf. Cooper, 1946, p. 724.

PATRILOCAL RESIDENCE AND THE UNILOCAL HOUSEHOLD

Araucanians find it difficult to generalize about the behavior patterns of kindred. This may well be due to the fact that they spend most of their lives within a rather circumscribed group of relatives. These are brought together through the workings of patrilocal residence customs, which still prevail almost without exception. It seems to have been the established rule for a young man to bring his bride to live in his father's house, thus leading to the formation of patrilocal, unilocal households. In the course of time, a married man of early middle age might find himself in the center of five generations which would include his father's father and his spouses, father and father's brothers and their respective mates, *ego's* brothers and their wives, *ego's* sons and their brides, his brothers' sons and their wives, his unmarried daughters, and *ego's* sons' children. Within such a group, *ego* would have exceedingly close ties with the members of his patrilineal lineage, for he and his father's father, and his son's son would all possess the same name, and his father's brothers would be surrogate fathers. Under normal conditions, a man would spend his entire life under his natal (paternal) roof, and his most intimate contacts would be with his housemates.

Men thus formed the more stable element of the society, since women had to forsake their natal households at marriage. Even in the case of females, however, household exogamy applied ordinarily only to first marriages, for a widow was very likely to marry one of her brothers-in-law, or else to be inherited by her son. In neither case would she have to leave her marital household.

Even at this date the Mapuche allow polygyny, and the custom was formerly widespread. With many males residing under a single roof, some limitation on spouses must have been maintained, and the number of wives a man could take seems to have been decided by the older men of the household.

Whereas the social structure clearly operated to promote masculine harmony and solidarity, it imposed great strains on women. They had scarcely any voice in the selection of mates, they had nothing to say about where they were going to live, and they had little expectation of being sole mistresses of their own households. That women were far from indifferent to this state of affairs may be judged by the manner in which they took advantage of an approved form of social singing to voice numerous complaints.[12] A newly married woman felt and acted like a stranger in her husband's household. She was expected not to plunge at once into the group's domestic affairs, and for several months she would sit facing the wall, without looking her housemates, other than her husband, directly in the face. Above all, she had to show great respect for her husband's father. To this day a woman is expected to show marked deference to adults of the other sex, particularly to her husband and father-in-law. Still, on two widely separated occasions I noted that men would not take it on themselves to sell objects belonging to their wives. When sales were made these women set the price and kept the money.

Not only did a bride have to make numerous adjustments to the men in her spouse's natal household, but she also had to learn to live harmoniously with the other women who had married into the same household. Particularly significant in this regard was the attitude of mutual distrust displayed by women who were married to brothers. Under the old system of unilocal, patrilocal residence, such sisters-in-law were forced to share a common residence, with all the tensions that this implies. These affinal relatives usually call each other by the special term *medomo*, the literal meaning of which is "feces woman." It is essential to understand that this is a conventional reciprocal term for coresident sisters-in-law, and is not merely an expletive used in anger or during a flash of hate.[13]

[12] Titiev, 1949, p. 16. Moesbach (1930, p. 240) described how older women comfort a recent bride and keep watch to prevent her from running away or injuring herself.

[13] Cf. Augusta, 1916, I: 133, and Titiev, 1949, pp. 9–11. The latter contains the texts of songs rendered by wives who are unhappy because they are mistreated by the husband's family, disregarded by a father-in-law, or distressed at the news that a husband's brother is about to bring a new bride into the household.

The warm feelings that link the natal coresidents of a household contrast sharply with the group's attitude toward outsiders. Commonly, latent hostility is expressed particularly toward the father's sister's husband, *kachü*, whose marriage deprives the natal unit of a member. *Kachü* is sometimes described as a potential traitor. As far as my data go, similar attitudes are not voiced toward other men who marry women of one's household.

Although the dictates of exogamy force the Araucanians to marry outside the natal household, they do not like to establish a wide range of affinal relationships. They tend to be fearful of strangers and to suspect them of being witches, so much so that boys used to be taught not to marry outsiders. When viewed in this light the customs of cross-cousin marriage and unilocal, patrilocal residence take on added significance. Under optimum conditions these practices require only two households for entrance into a series of marriage alliances. Thus, if a man brings home a wife from a certain outside household, his son secures a mate from the same group, since a woman and her brother's daughter belong to the same natal unit. In fact, the term *ñuke* (which applies to mother, mother's sister, and wife) may be said to connote woman of an affinal household. Nor should it be overlooked that sororate, sororal polygyny, and levirate all tend to maintain or strengthen marital ties that have already been established by two intermarrying groups.[14]

Latcham reached the conclusion that a rite called *konchotun* implied a system of matrimonial alliances between two families.[15] Others say only that *konchotun*, the central act of which called for the sacrifice and consumption of a sheep, was no more

[14] Although the analysis here proposed is based on information independently secured, it should be noted that Cooper (1946, p. 719) suggested a similar interpretation. He quoted statements to the effect that one native rationalized cross-cousin marriage on the basis that it prevented discord, and that an earlier writer stated that sororal polygyny was common " 'to avoid quarrels and jealousy.' "

[15] Latcham, 1924, p. 531.

than a declaration of friendship between two men, each of whom in turn provided a beast every other year.[16]

THE OMAHA SYSTEM: AN EVOLUTIONARY HYPOTHESIS

At the beginning of this chapter attention was drawn to the need for a dynamic approach to the study of Mapuche kinship. The necessity for an evolutionary analysis, which attempts to trace changes of form through the course of time, is nowhere more strikingly evident than when one tries to determine the presence or absence of Omaha nomenclature and patrilineal clans.

Ever since Hallowell tentatively identified Araucanian kinship terminology as Omaha,[17] many anthropologists have wanted to know whether his postulate is correct.[18] Anyone who studies the terms published by him and compares them with Figure 2 will soon find that Mapuche nomenclature is unquestionably Omaha. The following traits, male speaking, which are regarded as typical or diagnostic,[19] occur: parallel cousins are classed with siblings, father's sister's children are equated with sister's children, mother's brother's son is termed mother's brother or "uncle," and mother's brother's daughter is called mother.

As far as these essential features go, the Araucanians conform to Omaha usage. Much uncertainty has arisen, however, in regard to another trait which is commonly but not invariably associated with the Omaha system. The trait in dispute is marriage of a man with his wife's brother's daughter. Hallowell cited J. M. Collío to the effect that such marriages occur among the Araucanians, yet Hallowell stated that he failed to find confirmation of this fact in the literature;[20] and Cooper also noted

[16] Augusta, 1916, I: 93; Moesbach, 1930, pp. 389–91; and Housse, 1939, pp. 207–8.

[17] Hallowell, 1943.

[18] Hallowell's suggestion will be found to have been accepted by Cooper 1946, p. 724; and Murdock, 1949, p. 240.

[19] Lesser, 1929.

[20] Hallowell, 1943, p. 490.

that wife's brother's daughter marriage is nowhere else reported.[21] It so happens that I was privileged to work many long hours with J. M. Collío in Santiago, in 1948. Again and again, without revealing my purpose, I questioned him on this point, and invariably Collío denied the existence of the custom. In retrospect it seems to me that a single error of translation may be to blame for all the confusion. The Mapuche word *ñuke* means either wife or mother, and I venture the explanation that Collío sometimes spoke of marriage with wife's brother's daughter when he meant to say mother's brother's daughter, the traditional form of Araucanian cross-cousin marriage.

Even if the practice of marrying wife's brother's daughter is not recognized, however, enough parallels remain to justify the identification of the nomenclature as Omaha. Another interesting problem then arises, for it is widely held that Omaha terminology goes with fully developed patrilineal clans, but Mapuche society is not grouped into clans. For a consideration of this problem resort must be had to hypothesis, in the form of "historical" or "evolutionary" reconstruction.

A host of writers beginning with Lewis H. Morgan have argued that the various parts of a kinship system, such as terminology or marriage customs, do not necessarily originate, evolve, or change at one and the same time or rate of speed within a given social structure. Consequently, in some cases, "a recently acquired custom may not yet have developed an appropriate nomenclature, while [in other cases] . . . the nomenclature may survive after the custom has become obsolete.[22] The best understanding of the Araucanian situation can be gained when it is viewed in the light of a concept of nonsynchronous evolution.

An attempt will now be made to formulate a hypothesis with respect to the evolutionary development of the Mapuche kinship system. If one accepts the findings of Latcham, who

[21] Cooper, 1946, p. 719.

[22] Lowie, 1929, p. 173.

has put forward the most ambitious reconstruction of ancient Araucanian society, it may be postulated that before Spanish contacts gained full force, say prior to 1600, the Araucanians were divided into numerous matrilineal, totemic clans.[23] Unfortunately, Latcham's arguments are not always convincing, and his reasoning tends to be labored, but he has collected enough satisfactory evidence to demonstrate the likelihood that early historic Mapuche society had a matrilineal bias. Latcham also argued for a general habit of matrilocal residence,[24] an assumption that helps to explain the occurrence of a mother-in-law tabu.

Between about 1600 and 1900, as Latcham suggested, Araucanian society went through a transition from matrilineal to strongly patrilineal forms, coupled with the stringent practice of patrilocal residence. Much of this period, it should be recalled, was devoted to continuous warfare. Against this background Murdock's general remarks on the evolution of social organization are highly appropriate in their application to the specific case of the Mapuche. "Patrilocal residence," said Murdock, "seems to be promoted by any change in culture . . . which significantly enhances the status, importance, and influence of men in relation to the opposite sex. . . . War enhances men's influence and brings them captive (and hence patrilocal) wives and plunder wherewith to buy other women."[25] Murdock also pointed out that "anything which favors polygyny likewise favors the development of patrilocal residence."[26]

Thus, the era of steady fighting may be said to correspond roughly to the phase when Araucanian social organization was most strongly weighted on the masculine side. This was the time when the unilocal, patrilocal household group was the essential unit of society, and when a local chief's status was measured, presumably, in terms of the number of patrilineal

[23] Latcham, 1924, pp. 295–356, *et passim*. Also, see Guevara, 1929, I: 261 ff.

[24] Latcham, 1924, p. 360.

[25] Murdock, 1949, pp. 206–7.

[26] *Ibid.*

kin he had at his command. These conditions provide the socio-cultural milieu that is most congenial to the Omaha system, for it has already been established that Omaha nomenclature flourishes when a patrilineate is in its most highly developed form.[27]

There still remains for consideration the question of whether the Araucanians had a clan system at this stage of their history. On this score the literature is particularly baffling, for terms like clan, lineage, and family have been used with such varied connotations that they are worthless from the viewpoint of precise analysis. A reader can find a tremendous assortment of hints, possibilities, parallels, and suggestions that point to the existence of patrilineal clans,[28] but he searches in vain for an unequivocal account of Araucanian clanship, past or present. None the less, the absence of clans does not invalidate the existence and functioning of the Omaha system for, as I have maintained, there are times when unilocal household groups may be the exact equivalents of lineages or clans.[29]

Settlement on reservations, pacification, and the allotment of land in severalty must have had a serious impact on Araucanian social structure. The key to the shifts brought about by changed conditions may well have been the termination of the old system of unilocal, patrilocal residence, and its replacement by individual, neolocal habitations. Once again Murdock has provided an excellent conceptual framework for this discussion. He has stated that rules of residence are most vulnerable to outside forces and that they are often followed by loss of a clan system and, more slowly, by different descent regulations. Most resistant to change is kinship terminology.

"The development of neolocal residence, in societies following other rules," wrote Murdock in a passage directly relevant to the Araucanians, "appears to be favored by any influence which tends to isolate or to emphasize the individual or the

[27] White, 1939, pp. 569–70; Murdock, 1949, p. 240.

[28] Particularly revealing in this respect is the discussion of the *kuga* in Cooper, 1946, pp. 722–23.

[29] Titiev, 1943, pp. 518–19; 1944, pp. 46–48.

nuclear family."[30] Specifically, Murdock mentioned in this regard widespread poverty which inhibits wife purchase, Christian religious principles that forbid polygyny, the concept of private property and its attendant independence, and a shift of inheritance customs from primogeniture to division among a number of heirs.[31] Nearly every one of these modifications and influences has been at work among the Mapuche, with the consequence that their clan system, if they actually had one, has been destroyed; their unilocal, patrilocal household units are no longer maintained; levirate, sororate, and other polygynous arrangements are practically nonexistent; cross-cousin marriage has become a rarity; and yet the old Omaha terminology persists, having survived in spite of drastic changes of marriage, descent, and residence practices.

UNILOCAL HOUSEHOLDS AND POLITICAL UNITS

At no time in their recorded history do the Araucanians seem to have had anything like a formal and comprehensive political structure. When they were fighting major campaigns, they elected supreme commanders and lesser officers at public assemblies of adult males. The orders of these leaders were obeyed throughout the range of the entire tribe. Apparently, such large-scale organization was regarded as an emergency measure for, with the coming of peace, administrative controls reverted to the heads of small local units.[32] Never was there a continuously functioning tribal authority that had jurisdiction in times of peace, nor is there any record of true legislating bodies or procedures. Such "laws" as existed were not precisely formulated, and amounted to no more than traditional usages. Natives refer to them as *admapu* ("customs of the land"[33]) or as *piam* ("it is said"[34]) in the sense of sayings handed down by the ancestors. Even the most widely distributed of these beliefs and practices,

[30] Murdock, 1949, p. 203.

[31] *Ibid.*, pp. 201–8.

[32] See the treatment of this topic in Cooper, 1946, p. 724.

[33] Molina, 1808, II: 56; Augusta, 1916, I: 1.

[34] Augusta, 1916, I: 178.

however, were not necessarily in force throughout the entire tribal domain. And yet it cannot be said that the Mapuche lived in a state of anarchy.

Apparently, the principal weight of political authority ran along lines of kinship, and the unilocal household seems to have been the central element in the system. Each household comprised a localized and permanent succession of males, supplemented essentially by their wives and unmarried daughters. In the area south of the Cautín River the entire group, consisting of as many as eighty people, lived literally under a single roof;[35] north of the Cautín the unilocal arrangement was observed only in principle, inasmuch as three or four successive generations of men would build small, but independent *rukas* in close proximity to one another. These clusters are known as *lov*, *lof*, or *lofche*,[36] and in the aggregate their occupants comprise the same kin that lived in one large dwelling.

Each of the localized kinship groups was essentially autonomous when no major fighting was taking place. Normally, one of the oldest men held the position of chief, *loñko*, and at his death the office descended to his son, brother, or paternal nephew as the surviving men of the unit decided. It was the chief who held at least nominal title to his group's land, and it was he who allotted parts for the use of particular followers.[37] His advice was sought on all occasions, and no man of his unilocal household or its equivalent could marry without his consent. He was also expected to supervise payment of *llañkan* that involved his retainers. *Llañkan* was a form of restitution or wergild which had to be paid by a murderer to the survivors

[35] Latcham, 1924, p. 263. A description of a large unilocal household, with partitions separating the quarters assigned to a man's married sons, occurs in Smith, 1855, p. 295.

[36] It is interesting to speculate on the precise significance of these words. Augusta (1916, I: 116) translated *lof* as "break" or "collapse." I am tempted to think that the word applies to an aggregate of households that represents the breakdown of an older system of strictly unilocal residence. Latcham (1924, p. 263) used the word *lov* for these groups of structures.

[37] Cf. Smith, 1855, p. 241.

of his victim, by a man who abducted a bride without previous arrangement, by a lover who took another man's wife, or by the husband or family of a witch who happened to escape the death sentence. Under certain conditions, too, *llañkan* had to be paid to his affinal relatives by a spouse whose wife had died, even if the husband was not blamed for her death.

Nevertheless, despite his weighty responsibilities, the authority of a *loñko* was strictly limited. For the most part, he served only as the representative and spokesman of his unit, and he was expected to hold frequent assemblies of his adult, masculine followers, *kon·as,* in order to determine their wishes in advance.[38] Because of this custom a chief's power depended largely on his ability to sway his men through the skillful use of oratory.[39] He was also esteemed in proportion to his wealth in terms of land, herds, wives, and household goods. To some extent, the welfare of the people was supposed to depend on the leaders, for it was widely believed that the advent of evil times presaged the death of a prominent man.

If a chief died or if his *kon·as* wished to depose him, neighboring caciques were called in to supervise the choice of a new leader. A large assembly of the men concerned was held, and all principals or their spokesmen were given a thorough hearing. When all had spoken, the presiding chiefs selected as the new *loñko* the candidate who seemed to have the best qualifications and the greatest support of his prospective retainers. There was no fixed policy of tenure for the chief, but, unless he aroused tremendous opposition, he usually served for life.

Molina wrote that the Araucanian "state" was partitioned into four independent districts called *uthal-mapu*, each of which was led by a *toqui*. Every *uthal-mapu* was divided into five "provinces" and each of these in turn was subdivided into nine "counties" presided over by *ulmens*.[40] Several early sources re-

[38] Cf. Smith, 1855, pp. 241–43; Moesbach, 1930, pp. 122–38; and Edwards, 1930, 14 ff.

[39] See Moesbach, 1930, p. 126; and Cooper, 1946, p. 737.

[40] Molina, 1808, II: 55–56.

ferred to similar sociopolitical structures, but their data are too fragmentary and their terminology too inconsistent to provide a clear presentation.[41] All authors agree on two points. Whatever the true nature of the system may have been, it functioned best in times of war; and the smaller units were autonomous except during emergencies.

From a review of all the known facts it seems evident that far beyond all other considerations, a local chief's prestige depended on the number of able-bodied men at his disposal. Even when they were nominally at peace the Araucanians frequently carried out intratribal raids, known as *malones*.[42] In this practice the political and kinship systems merge into one, for the size of a *loñko's* following depended primarily on the number of sons he and the men of his lineage begot. That explains why polygyny was so widely practiced and why great chiefs commonly amassed as many as twenty wives apiece.[43] Almost invariably, the authority of a *loñko* was restricted to kinfolk, and the central core of his following was formed by those members of his patrilineal lineage who would have resided in his household under the ancient scheme of unilocal, patrilocal residence. It is significant that during an interview on this subject Juan Antinao voluntarily defined a *loñko* as *la cabeza de la familia y su reducción*.[44] Such an interpretation is also supported by the fact that chiefs are known whose following numbered only 120 to 130 persons.[45]

Under the traditional form of Araucanian social organization, each chief was assisted by two important officials called *werkens*.

[41] Cooper, 1946, p. 725. Latcham (1924) devoted his fifth and sixth chapters to lengthy discussions of these supposed sociopolitical units, but throughout he stressed their ceremonial or totemic implications.

[42] Latcham (1909, p. 354): "Armed raids (*malones*) were constantly made on the neighboring villages. . . ." A vivid description of a large-scale attack occurs in Moesbach, 1930, pp. 270–87.

[43] Latcham, 1909, p. 359.

[44] Similar statements to the effect that chiefs had authority only over kin may be found in numerous places. See, for example, Latcham, 1909, pp. 356–57; Edwards, 1930, p. 13; and Cooper, 1946, p. 726.

[45] Housse, 1939, pp. 249 and 282.

They were his heralds or trusted messengers and were used particularly for carrying on negotiations with other head men. They had to have excellent memories in order to transmit messages precisely, and it was necessary for them to be good orators so that they could deliver their communications effectively.[46] They traveled in pairs to check the exactness of each other's statements, and in the hope that one of them could get through to a destination even if his partner were waylaid or killed. A clever *werken* was likely to be chosen to replace a deceased *loñko,* and it is altogether probable that service as a herald was considered the best training for a future chief.

The traditional system of chieftainship, whatever may have been its vicissitudes in times past, received a deathblow when the practice of allotting reservation lands in severalty began. At the beginning of the reservation period, when each recognized chief of a kinship unit (presumably a *lof*) was given a *título de merced* on behalf of his group, the position of *loñko* seemed to be strengthened. When, however, one reduction after another was subdivided and titles were distributed to particular landowners, chieftainship lost its main support. As more and more individuals acquired their own property, they tended to follow their own inclinations without seeking the advice of elders; and as more and more homesteads were built on separate land holdings, the older pattern of large unilocal residences disappeared. Furthermore, partly through government and missionary pressure, and partly because they no longer have a monopoly of wealth, chiefs cannot indulge in large-scale polygyny and can no longer hope to beget large numbers of followers. Such as it was, the old order of chieftainship is gone, and no new form of leadership has yet emerged.[47]

[46] Examples of the style in which *loñkos* and *werkens* spoke may be found in Augusta, 1934, pp. 9–13.

[47] Occasionally, a politically conscious Araucanian is a candidate for national office on a platform designed to win the support of his fellow tribesmen. A few Araucanian deputies have been elected, but rural natives regard them with suspicion.

RESERVATION SOCIAL STRUCTURE

In no province of Araucanian culture is there such a dearth of information as there is with regard to the social composition of a typical reduction. The Mapuche term for a reservation, *trokiñche*, does not throw much light on the problem, as it has no deeper meaning than "an assemblage of people." It was for the purpose of supplying some of the missing information that the first few weeks of intensive field work were devoted primarily to a study of Cautinche's social structure. This reservation was selected as the first base of operations because a preliminary visit had indicated that it was well suited to such a purpose. It is moderately small and lies far enough away from Cholchol to preserve much of its aboriginal quality. Moreover, we were made welcome by the Reverend Juan Antinao and his family, and were permitted to place our caravan in the center of a group of homesteads (Fig. 4). Juan Antinao, the present holder of Cautinche's *título de merced*, is the son of the former *loñko* of the community. He has lived at Cautinche all his life, and he was able to supply many essential data about every one of the reservation's inhabitants.

As the study progressed, we discovered that Cautinche had been founded by a pioneer from Carrarriñe. It developed that the two reservations had other ties in common, which led us to move to Carrarriñe as soon as the detailed analysis of Cautinche had been completed. In due course we learned that Carrarriñe had important links with Renaco. For that reason we decided to investigate Renaco on the completion of the study of Carrarriñe.

This chapter, then, consists of detailed analyses of the social structures of Cautinche, Carrarriñe, and Renaco, with a number of general ideas that arose in the course of the work. Cautinche was the most thoroughly investigated as circumstances did not permit equal attention to all three reservations.

GEOGRAPHICAL SETTING

The district which contains the three reservations lies between the Nahuelbuta coastal mountains on the west and the slopes of the Andes on the east. This area is characterized by many picturesquely rounded hills, no one of which rises very high above sea level. Throughout much of the year one may see in the distance as many as eight snow-capped volcanic peaks on the eastern horizon, among them the renowned Llaima and Villarica. One outstanding feature of this zone is the Cautín River Valley, and another is the valley of the Cholchol. The Cholchol River and its tributaries flow through much of the region under study, and at Neuva Imperial the Cholchol joins the main branch of the Cautín (Map 2).

Most of the trade contacts of Cautinche, Carrarriñe, and Renaco are with the Chilean community at Cholchol, which can be reached by unimproved dirt roads. A considerable amount of traffic goes by oxcart in dry weather, but in the rainy winter months travel is limited to horseback. Many transactions also take place in Nueva Imperial, which is a much larger commercial center than Cholchol. This city may be reached in the usual fashion, except for the need of crossing the Cholchol River at Los Boldos (Map 2). A flat raft, pulled hand over hand along a steel cable by passengers and "crew" (Pl. V, Fig. 2), makes necessary crossings, except when the river is in flood. Nueva Imperial is situated on the branch line of a railroad that connects with the main line at Temuco, a thriving frontier city of more than 40,000 inhabitants, which is the capital of Cautín Province and is the largest business center in the territory under consideration. Indians from many neighboring reservations visit Temuco regularly, and in fair weather it can be reached from Cholchol by horseback in four to five hours and by oxcart in less than a day. A few trucks and an occasional automobile travel between Cholchol and Temuco with passengers and freight, when road conditions permit. In May, 1948, members of the Temuco flying club began to provide occasional air service to and from Cholchol in a small, single-engined plane. A large crowd gathered on the town's soccer field (Pl. VI, Fig. 2) to watch the landing of the plane when Miss Dorothea Royce, head of the Misión Araucana's hospital, became the first passenger to fly out of Cholchol. Thereafter, for the few who could avail themselves of the service, Cholchol became only fifteen

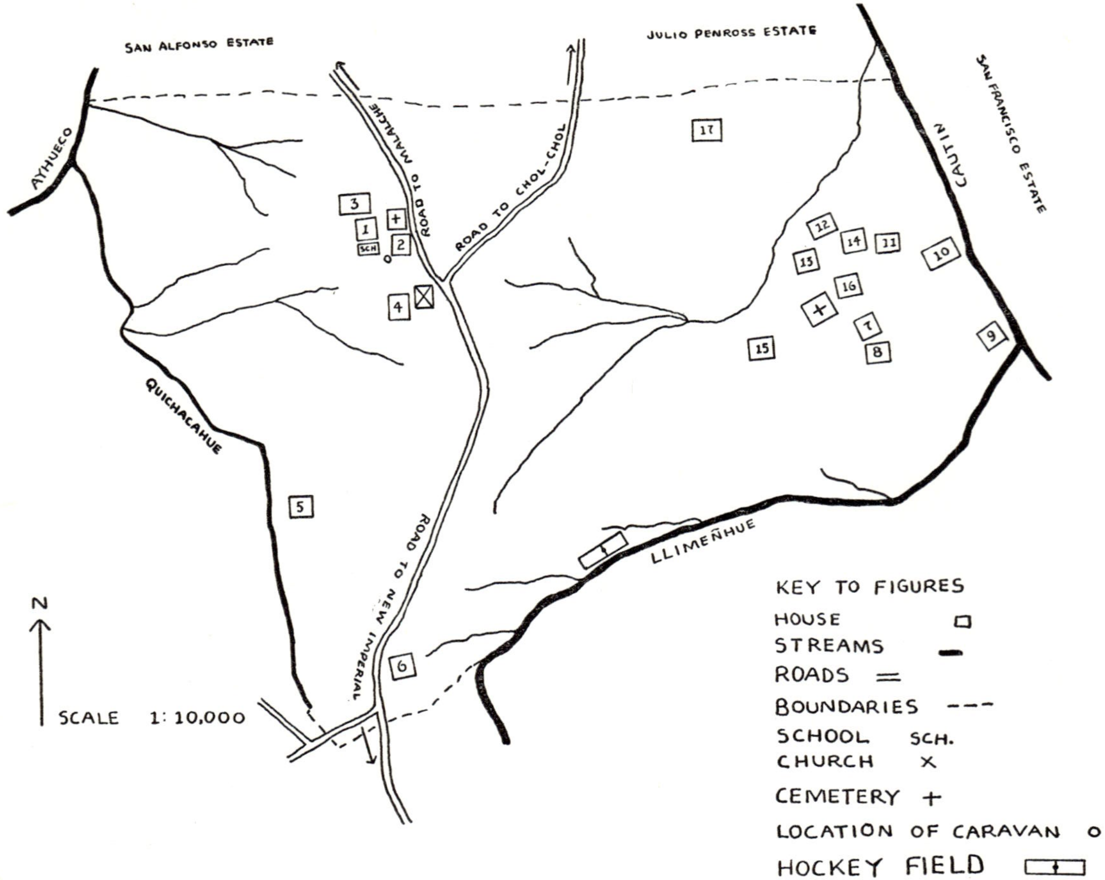

FIG. 4. Cautinche settlement pattern. Based on an original field sketch made by Raúl González. The key also applies to Figures 8 and 9.

minutes distant from Temuco, and soon the Indians scarcely looked up when they heard a plane in the sky.[1]

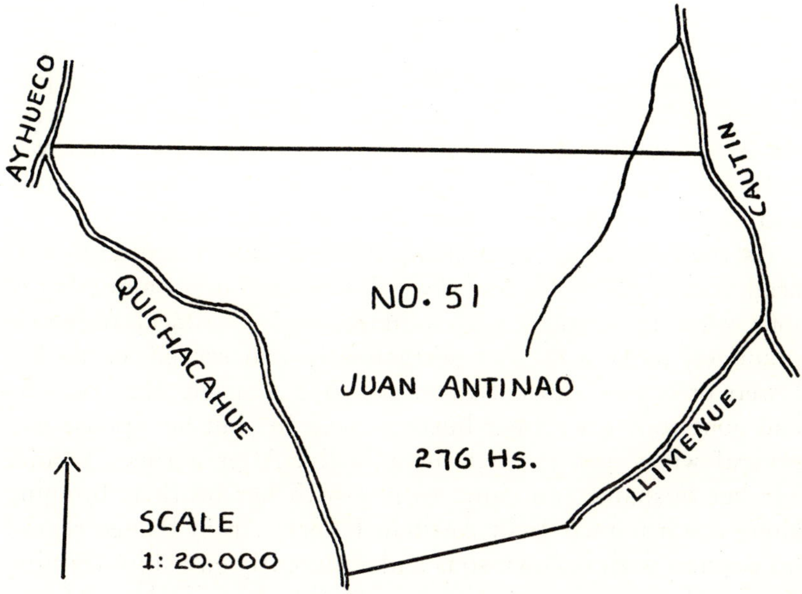

FIG. 5. *Título de Merced* for Cautinche, 1893. Based on an original map in the possession of Juan Antinao. Stream names have been added for purposes of identification of boundaries. The original failed to mark off precise limits.

HISTORICAL SKETCH OF CAUTINCHE

Until a century or so ago, the district now called Cautinche had no human occupants. At some time just before 1850 a Carrarriñe man named Antío Paineo built a house near the

[1] The Reverend Mr. Crawford, a Methodist missionary in Nueva Imperial, flies his own small plane to many reservations in the vicinity. When Raúl González and I were scheduled to leave the field on July 27, 1948, the Cholchol River was in flood, and we were faced with the prospect of a long, circuitous horseback ride in the rain. Luckily, a break in the weather gave us a chance to call for a plane. In the space of about an hour a pilot made two round trips, flying us from Cholchol to Temuco one at a time. Our baggage followed by oxcart.

Cautín River, not far from house No. 13 on Figure 4. For this reason the settlement came to be known as Cautinche ("people of Cautín"). There are conflicting stories concerning Antío Paineo's reason for moving away from Carrarriñe. Some say that he was driven out for misconduct, but others claim that he was only an alert pioneer who took advantage of an opportunity to lay claim to a good piece of virgin territory. Cautinche's founder chose wisely, for he picked a spot that was both well watered and well drained and that unquestionably had excellent forest and plant cover in those days.

As the founder of Cautinche, Antío Paineo became its first head man or *loñko*. He had several wives and begot a number of sons who, in keeping with unilocal and patrilocal residence practices, lived with him permanently and served as his followers or *kon·as*. Antío Paineo also had a sister, Jacinta, who had gone to live with her husband near by, but her spouse had several wives and treated them badly. After a time, Jacinta left her husband and came to live with her brother, bringing along a son named Juan Antinao Paineo. Antío Paineo reared his nephew with his own sons and apparently gave him training as a *werken* and a potential heir to the chieftainship. At any rate, when Antío Paineo died, his succession was disputed between his son, Dionisio Paillao and his sister's son, Juan Antinao Paineo. Although the son was traditionally favored to succeed, he was judged in council to lack the force of character and oratorical skill that were highly regarded in a leader, and Juan was elected *loñko*. He proved to be an able leader,[2] and during the period when reservations were being formed he was given an official *título de merced* on December 19, 1893, that entitled him to 276 hectares for the use of forty-four kinfolk (see Fig. 5). One gathers that Dionisio Paillao and some of his brothers were not satisfied to have their late father's prerogatives transferred to a nephew, for they soon began to leave the paternal roof and to build separate homes of their own. Since no one in those days had a precisely defined individual plot of ground, much

[2] While the main facts of the story are doubtless correct, it should be borne in mind that this narrative was told by Juan Antinao Paineo's son.

bickering arose as the community expanded, and accusations of trespass were bandied back and forth. Very likely the situation became worse when Juan Antianao Paineo died and left the Cautinche title to his son, the present Reverend Juan Antinao. At that time Juan was not yet converted to Christianity, and he was much given to drink. Things grew worse

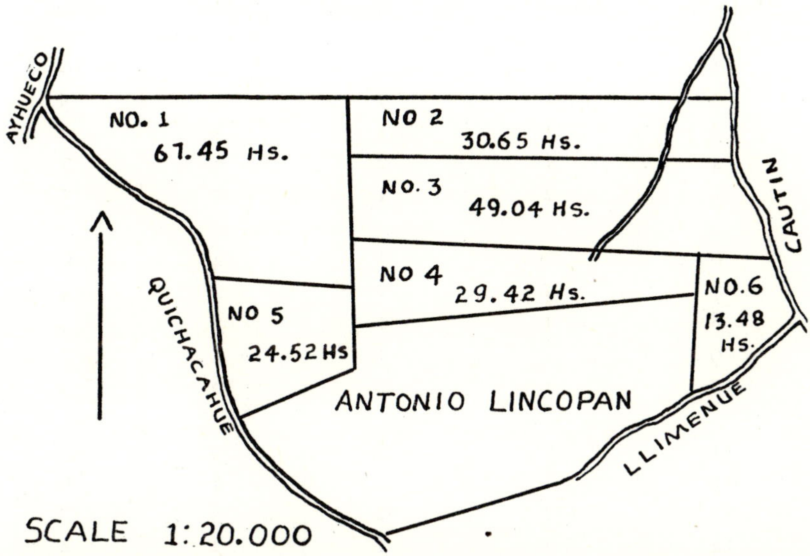

FIG. 6. Cautinche allotments in 1917. From an original drawing owned by Juan Antinao. As in Figure 5, precise boundaries are not established. Antonio Lincopan, who unlike other holders is named but not numbered, received 61.44 hectares.

and worse, and incessant quarreling threatened to disrupt the settlement. At last it was decided to petition the Chilean authorities to subdivide Cautinche and to allot land in severalty to specific owners. The reservation was partitioned on November 12, 1917 (Fig. 6). Juan Antinao received 67.45 hectares and promptly built himself a new home on his own land (house No. 1 on Fig. 4). Thereafter, other householders followed suit until Cautinche took on its current appearance, as shown in Figure 4.

SOCIAL COMPOSITION OF CAUTINCHE

In 1948 the reduction consisted of 111 people who were distributed among seventeen houses (Table II).

TABLE II

DISTRIBUTION OF CAUTINCHE'S POPULATION[3]

House No.	Adult Men	Adult Women	Children	Total
1	1	1	8	10
2	1	1	3	5
3	1	1	2	4
4	1	2	4	7
5	2	1	2	5
6	1	1	4	6
7	1	1	2	4
8	1	0	3	4
9	1	1	1	3
10	1	2	6	9
11	2	2	9	13
12	1	1	4	6
13	2	2	3	7
14	1	1	2	4
15	1	1	4	6
16	1	1	3	5
17	1	2	10	13
Totals	20	21	70	111

Two households contain as many as thirteen inmates each, and one has as few as three, but the average is six and one-half.

[3] The house numbers follow the scheme used in Figure 4. The system of numbering is entirely arbitrary and is used simply for convenience in making references.

Readers are reminded that statistical data obtained from natives are not always entirely accurate.

Every dwelling has at least one child, and only a single household lacks an adult woman. No more than three residences shelter two adult men, which indicates that there are no long-standing bachelors and which also serves to show how little is left of the traditional unilocal household system. There are very few spinsters and no unmarried widows or divorcees.

TABLE III

NATAL RESERVATIONS OF CAUTINCHE WIVES

Present Wives	Former Wives	Total	Natal Reservation
6	2	8	Carrarriñe
3	2	5	Boldoche
1	3	4	Romulwe
1	2	3	Cautinche
1	2	3	Chivilcoyam
0	2	2	Denencuhue
0	2	2	Malalche
0	1	1	Huichicon
1	0	1	Coigue
0	1	1	Curaco
1	0	1	Peyuko
1	0	1	Pemuche
1	0	1	Catrimalal
1	0	1	Cuelche
Totals 17	17	34	

The practice of polygyny still exists, but seems to be falling into disuse. It was reported that in the recent past men with two or three wives occupied houses Nos. 5, 7, 10, 11, and 17,[4] but at present only occupants of Nos. 4, 10, and 11 are reported to have two wives each. It is worthwhile to analyze the marriage arrangements a bit more, in the light of the general discussion in the preceding chapter. At one time or another the seventeen male householders have married a total of thirty-four women.

[4] Doubtless, Cautinche's first two *loñkos* had multiple wives but, since exact information was unobtainable, they are not included in this discussion.

Of these, only three were from Cautinche (Table III), which strongly suggests that at Cautinche reservation exogamy is the rule. The men do not seem to have ranged too far afield in the quest for mates, for all of the reservations listed in Table III are close together (see Fig. 1). Nearly half of the wives, sixteen out of thirty-four, came either from the parent reduction of Carrarriñe or from the intervening communities of Chivilcoyam and Boldoche (see Fig. 1). This seems to indicate a preference for making marital arrangements among a restricted number of social units.

A review of the past and present polygynous matings also throws light on the operation of the social system. Thus, Juan Llancanao Antinao, of house No. 4 (Fig. 4), was first married to a Carrarriñe woman and about seven years later he took a second wife from the same reservation. The original occupant of house No. 5, Huenchual Huenupi, married a woman from Romulwe, by whom he had seven children. He also took another mate from Romulwe, by whom he begot three children. On the death of his first wife Huenchual Huenupi went to Argentina, but his second spouse remained in Cautinche with a lover. On Huenchual's return home his wife and her lover moved to Argentina. Huenchual never remarried.

Millan Lincopan, of house No. 7, married his first wife some forty-five years ago, took a second mate about five years later, and a third after the lapse of a similar period. All three women shared the same *ruka* for many years. They are said to have quarreled in the beginning, but to have lived in harmony after a time. The first and third spouses were distant relatives from Denencuhue, but the second woman was unrelated to them and was from Romulwe. Millan Lincopan had offspring by all three wives. After their death he married a widow from Boldoche, by whom he had one son.

Householder No. 10, Antonio Huircapan, was married to two women through the levirate, as each of them was the widow of an older brother. Moreover, in accord with traditional usage, they were cross-cousins (*ñuke*) of their husbands.[5] Another

[5] The man in house No. 16 also acquired his wife by levirate.

polygynous household, No. 11, was maintained by Antonio Huircapan's half brother, Domingo. At one time Domingo was wedded to three wives, the first of whom he inherited from a deceased brother. In house No. 17 there lived a man who married two unrelated women by whom he begot five and six children, respectively.

Despite the presence of a native pastor and an Episcopal church, only the couples in houses Nos. 1, 2, and 10 have had church weddings. All the rest were married by customary Araucanian rites, in addition to which the householders in houses Nos. 3, 4, 8, and 15 have gone through Chilean civil ceremonies.[6] Probably because of opposition from the church there is no active medicine woman, *machi*, at Cautinche. There is a hockey field where games are sometimes played, but none of the traditional religious ceremonies is held. Maria Munos, wife of Pedro Llancao in house No. 9, is a trained *machi*. She came to Cautinche about ten years ago when, as an elderly widow, she married Pedro. I was told that her professional services are rarely or never called for, and she does not even have the notched post, *rewe*, which is the essential sign of a practicing *machi* (contrast Pl. VII, Figs. 1 and 2).

Although the direct authority of the church over Cautinche and its environs does not appear very great, it exerts a good deal of influence indirectly through its school. The Cautinche school, conducted under the auspices of the Misión Araucana, is taught by Juan Antinao's son. Whenever the teacher is otherwise engaged his sister, Josephina, conducts class. Pupils are drawn from several reservations (Table IV).

Ability to speak Spanish is the most striking accomplishment of the school children. In addition, youngsters learn to read a little and to do elementary arithmetic. Of Cautinche's adult population, however, it was estimated by Juan Antinao that ten men and six women spoke fluent Spanish, while the rest had only a smattering of the language.

[6] The Reverend Juan Antinao will marry in church only monogamous couples or the first wife of a polygynous husband. He will baptize any child whose parents have had either a church or civil wedding.

One must not lose sight of the fact that Cautinche was first settled by a unilocal, patrilocal group which retained its essential structure for some time. Even today the reservation may be regarded, broadly speaking, as a sort of multilocal, patrilineal kinship group. With a single exception, all the men are related. Occupants of houses Nos. 1, 2, 4, 7, 8, 10, 11, 12, 13, and 15 trace their ancestry back to Juan Antinao Paineo, and the owners of houses Nos. 3, 5, 9, 16, and 17 to his cousin, Dionisio Paillao. Only the occupant of No. 14, Oligario Nankucheyo, is genealogically unconnected with the others. He first came to

TABLE IV

CAUTINCHE SCHOOL ROSTER

Home Reservation	Boys	Girls	Total
Cautinche	12	9	21
Denencuhue	6	8	14
Curaco	2	2	4
Boldoche	3	0	3
Catrimalal	0	2	2
Ayehueco	0	1	1
Huichicon	0	1	1
Totals[7]	23	23	46

Cautinche as a laborer for his wife's uncle, Antonio Huircapan, of house No. 10, and now works for him on half shares. Oligario Nankucheyo moved from the Yauyahuenche subdivision of Malalche, his home reservation, because he had no land of his own. He and his wife may be called the only "immigrants" in Cautinche. They arrived about three years ago and have become so well adjusted that they are liked by all their neighbors.

[7] Although forty-six pupils are shown on the official roster, half of the number generally missed attendance, and some "students" probably never came to class. Since teachers are paid on the basis of enrollments, there is a tendency to exaggerate the size of a school's roster.

One other case that is somewhat irregular because it involves an instance of matrilocal residence deserves mention. Santiago Huircan, owner of House No. 6, is only distantly related to Cautinche's founder. He was born in Catrimalal and lived there until about 1938. At that time his wife, who is the daughter of Juan Antinao's brother, inherited some eighteen hectares at Cautinche. Thereupon, the couple moved to Cautinche and Santiago began to farm on his wife's land. There is no feeling of strangeness towards this family, and they have been completely accepted by the Cautinche community.

HISTORY AND DESCRIPTION OF CARRARRIÑE

Like Cautinche, Carrarriñe lies between Chile's coastal ranges and the Andes, and its topography also is featured by gently sloping hills. Here the major drainage is provided by the Cholchol River, which runs close by the eastern boundary of the reservation. Several streamlets flow across the area, and in the rainy season the low-lying lands are often flooded. There are many indications of aboriginally dense forest cover, but the region is currently bare of trees except where groves of eucalyptus or apple orchards have recently been planted (Frontispiece). Unimproved dirt roads connect Carrarriñe with Nueva Imperial and Cholchol.

Carrarriñe is a much larger reduction than is Cautinche. It contains 1,438 hectares, officially known as parcel or *hijuela* 54 (see Fig. 7). Title to this land is in the name of Antonio Painemal, who is accordingly the nominal chief. Two adjacent reservations, Picuta and Tromenguelo (Figs. 7, 8), are so closely linked with Carrarriñe that all three may be regarded as comprising a kind of "Greater Carrarriñe."[8] It was not possible to ascertain the true nature of the relationships that exist among the three districts, but it appears likely that division occurred at one time or another when reservation boundaries and land titles were being regularized. A former Carrarriñe man, Mulato Chihuaihuen, is said to have set himself up as an independent

[8] That part of Coigue which is shown on Figure 7 is also said by some informants to be part of "Greater Carrarriñe."

chief of Tromenguelo almost a century ago. At an unspecified date Rosario Morales, a Chilean interpreter who spoke fluent Mapuche, is believed to have taken advantage of his government connections to acquire title to the 480 hectares that make up Picuta. Nowadays, both Tromenguelo and Picuta have their

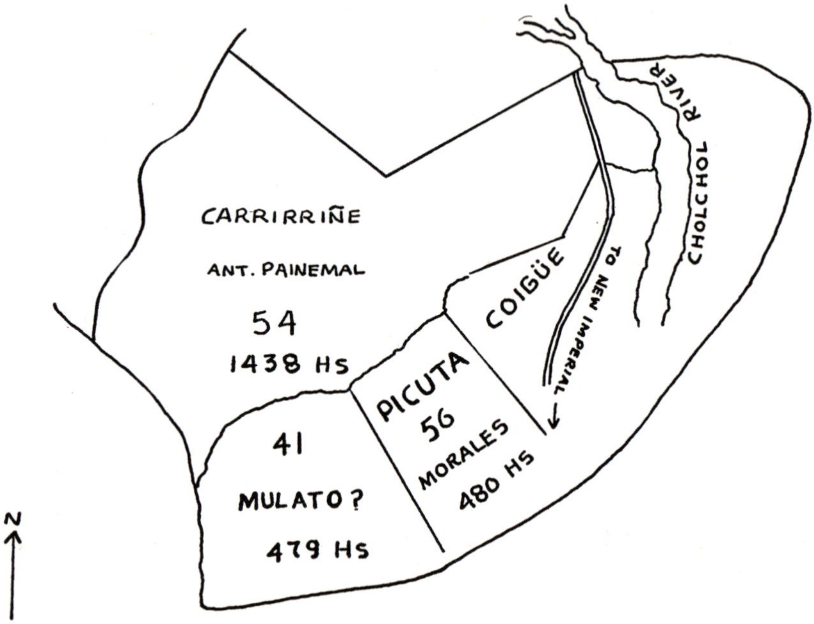

FIG. 7. *Título de Merced* for Carrarriñe. Redrawn from the original in the office of the Ministry of Lands and Colonization in Temuco. Parcels 41 and 56, known respectively as Tromenguelo and Picuta, seem to have been given reservation status at the request of former Carrarriñe residents.

own chiefs, hockey fields, and prayer grounds, and are regarded as independent reservations.[9]

There are two varying stories of Carrarriñe's founding. According to one version it was settled by a band which left Renaco because of overcrowding or on account of a quarrel over

[9] Somewhat similar divisions or three-in-one situations were reported for other communities, such as Malalche and Tranahuillín.

a woman. According to the other version a large group of Araucanians crossed the Andes from Argentina and settled at Nacimiento, near the upper reaches of the Bío Bío, or at Villarica, soon after 1800. Later, one unit went to Renaco while another moved into new territory at Carrarriñe. The name most commonly attributed to the latter's first settler is Manqueo who, accompanied by some brothers and other relatives, arrived around 1825. Two of his putative brothers were called Nahuelhual and Collío, and one of his daughters married a Painemal, from whom the reservation's present title holder is descended. One of Manqueo's sons, Paillao Huaiquian, succeeded his father as *loñko*, and founded the Huaiquian branch of the family, which is still important at Carrarriñe. One of his first cousins was known as Paineo, and he became the ancestor of another important family.

Today the principal groups at Carrarriñe are called Painemal, Huaiquian, Paineo, and Collío. All represent contemporaneous offshoots of Manqueo, the reservation's founder. Nevertheless, these people do not live in complete harmony, and at least three factions can be distinguished: Collío, Painemal, and Huaiquian-Paineo. The most obvious sign of the rift is in respect to hockey fields. These playing grounds are important because they are used not only for sport but also for major rituals. At Carrarriñe there are four separate fields. One, associated with the Huaiquian-Paineo group, is the main field and is recognized by all the inhabitants (Fig. 8, near house No. 25, and Pl. XI, Fig. 2). A second field, somewhat more restricted in use, is linked with the Collío family (Fig. 8, near house No. 18), and a third is associated with the Painemals (Fig. 8, near No. 6). Still another schism seems to have occurred in 1948, when Bartolo Gallardo put a new hockey field into use near his own home (Fig. 8, No. 38). Gallardo's action is linked with Carrarriñe's dispute over schools.

Approximately twelve years ago Bartolo Gallardo moved to Carrarriñe from Tromenguelo because he had inherited some land from his grandfather and because his mother was living in Carrarriñe. About 1938 Gallardo was appointed to teach in the

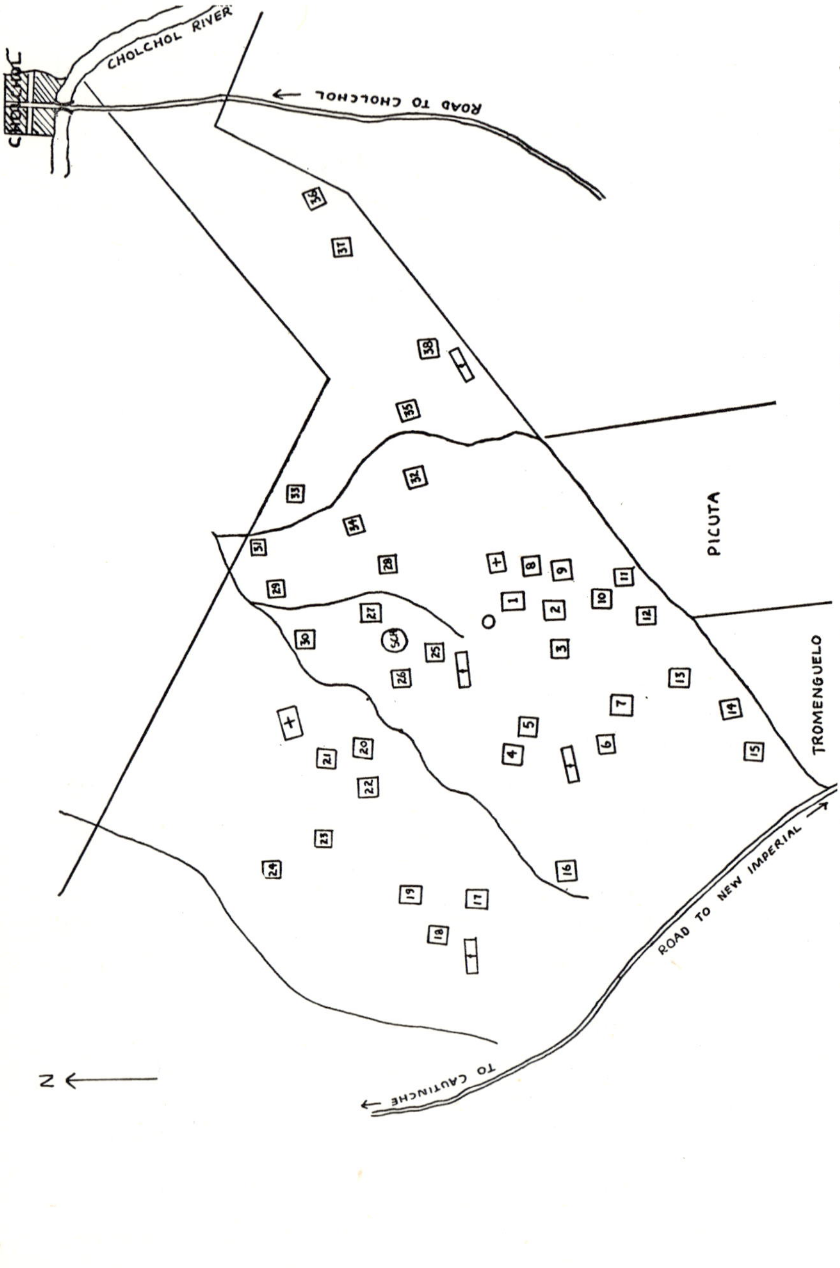

FIG. 8. Carrarriñe settlement pattern. Based on a diagram by Raúl González. Only the houses studied in the text are shown. The key to figures is the same as in Figure 4.

Misión Araucana's school at Carrarriñe. Soon after, a rival instructor named Martín Duminghual opened an independent school with government support. A series of quarrels broke out, and Carrarriñe became divided into parties that supported or opposed Gallardo. Early in 1948 the Misión Araucana found it necessary to dismiss Gallardo, who was replaced by Domingo Carilaf from Tranahuillín (Pl. XVI, Fig. 2). Thereupon, Gallardo opened a school of his own and dedicated a new hockey field on July 14, 1948. Thus, Carrarriñe finds itself in the curious position of harboring three schools within a league of one another.

SOCIAL COMPOSITION OF CARRARRIÑE

Carrarriñe was officially designated as a reduction in December, 1887, and underwent allotment on December 16, 1921. It contains between fifty and fifty-five households. Working conditions did not permit us to secure sociological data on all the inhabitants, but information was obtained for thirty-eight dwellings, distributed as indicated in Figure 8. There were 224 people residing in the thirty-eight units studied, an average of six to a household. The range is two to twelve, and the mode is six, as may be seen in Table V.

The social structure of Carrarriñe differs from that of Cautinche in several basic respects. For one thing, reservation exogamy is far less common, probably because the population of Carrarriñe is larger and more diversified. Data obtained for thirty-six married women reveal that thirteen, or 36 per cent, of them came from "Greater Carrarriñe," eleven from within the main reservation, and two from Tromenguelo. The remaining wives were drawn from many scattered reductions. Informants pointed out several polygynous households, but did not furnish adequate statistics. In one interesting case a native speaker treated as a single familial unit the members of a bigamous group in which a man's two wives lived in adjacent houses. In only one household (Fig. 8, No. 10) was there no adult woman. A widower and two unmarried sons kept house there.

TABLE V

Distribution of Carrarriñe's Population

House No.	No. of Occupants
1	4
2	6
3	6
4	7
5	3
6	3
7	4
8	9
9	4
10	3
11	5
12	9
13	4
14	6
15	5
16	2
17	6
18	6
19	6
20	3
21	12
22	10
23	5
24	7
25	8
26	3
27	3
28	6
29	8
30	3
31	12
32	6
33	6
34	6
35	7
36	3
37	10
38	8
Total	224

The absence of a church and resident pastor provides the basis for another contrast with Cautinche. Sunday services are conducted in the schoolhouse either by the local teacher or by a visiting member of the Misión Araucana's staff from Cholchol. A small number of Carrarriñe folk have had civil or church weddings, and much of the population has been baptized at one time or another, but one sees very little evidence of intense devotion to Christianity. Two active *machis* reside on the reservation (Fig. 8, No. 26),[10] and native ceremonies are held at intervals. Only a few of the older people speak fluent Spanish, and some of the others have no command of the language at all.

Thirty-five children, from seven to sixteen years of age, are registered in the main school taught by Domingo Carilaf. There are ten boys and nineteen girls from Carrarriñe and five boys and three girls from Boldoche (see Pl. XVI, Fig. 2). School matters play a prominent part in the internal affairs of the reduction. There is, or was, an Araucanian Educational Society that met regularly, at least between October, 1933, and August, 1947. It elected officers, collected dues, and made decisions with regard to the selection of teachers, location of buildings, procurement of equipment, and related matters. Women, as well as men, were enrolled as members, and the activities of the group are suggestive of PTA affairs in the United States.

In this reduction one of the most striking differences from Cautinche is the large number of unwed adults: five widowers, eleven widows, twenty-two spinsters, and twenty-six bachelors. This must not be interpreted to imply a high level of celibacy. A more realistic interpretation, suggested by informants, indicates that under the allotment system it is becoming increasingly difficult for young men to secure enough land to enable them to support wives and families. Also because of economic pressure, a few men and women annually leave the reservation to look for work in cities or on privately owned estates.

[10] The home of only one of the *machis* is shown in Figure 8. Her house and *rewe* are pictured (Pl. VII, Fig. 2).

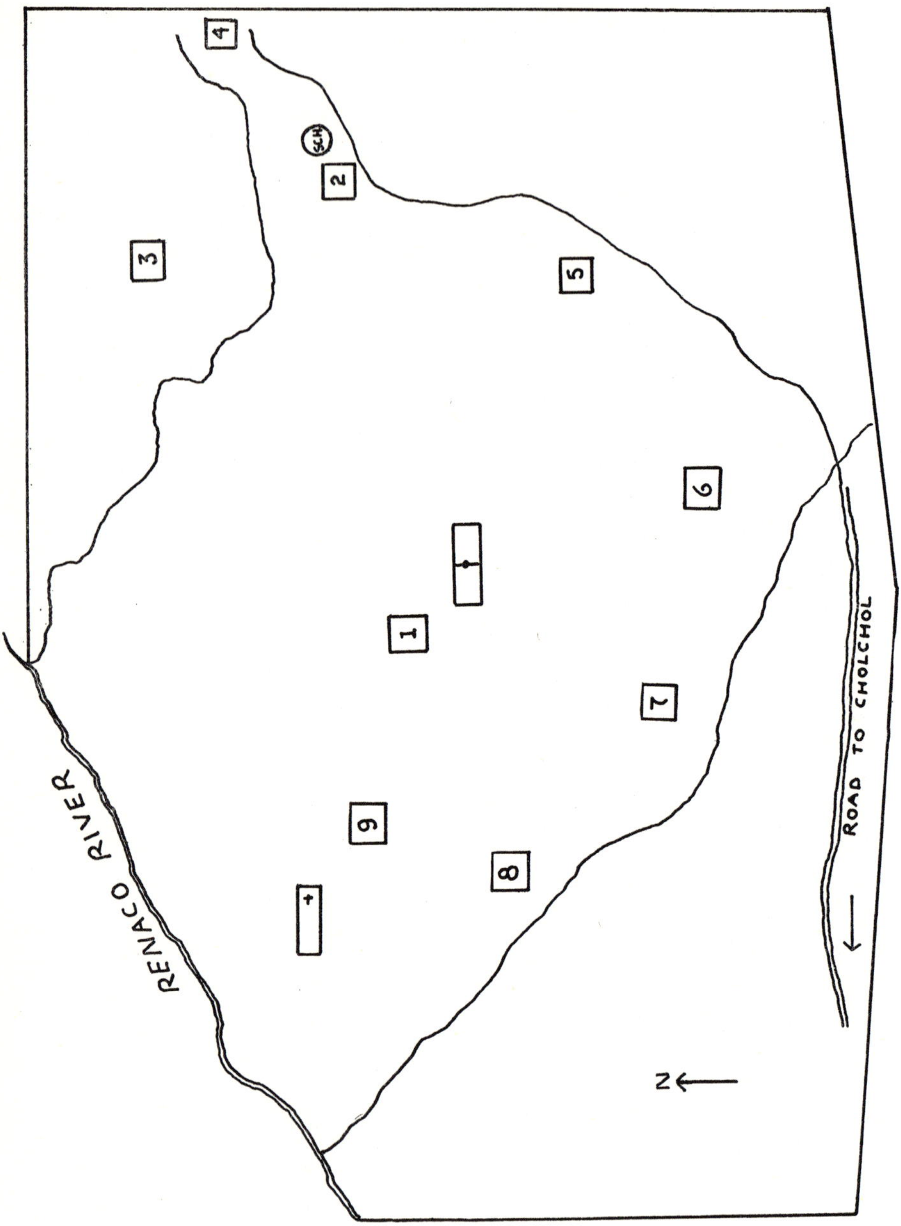

FIG. 9. Renaco settlement pattern. From a diagram by Raúl González. The hockey field near house No. 1 is distinct from the *ñillatun* ground near No. 9. See Figure 4 for key to symbols.

BACKGROUND AND DESCRIPTION OF RENACO

Renaco, a small reduction of 275 hectares, lies about four kilometers northeast of Cholchol. Title is held by the *loñko*, Fermín Nahuelhual. The terrain falls into two divisions, a hilly section that is part of the eastern foothills of the Nahuelbuta coastal range, and a flat meadow-like area which is drained by the Renaco stream that enters the Cholchol River at Cholchol. Since there are only nine houses, with a populace of fifty-six, it might seem that there is enough land for all, but much of the hilly ground is unsuited for growing wheat, and the lowland receives too much moisture to yield good crops.

Renaco was settled, probably in 1825, by Araucanians who had crossed the Andes from Argentina. The first family to arrive was that of Collío Huenchual, from whom the present chief is descended. All the householders now living on the reservation are members of a single large family. Three men have built homes in the hilly section (Fig. 9, Nos. 2, 4, 5), and the others are spread over the meadow, with the leader's house (Fig. 9, No. 1) more or less centrally located. As long ago as 1885 a traveler described Renaco as having six to eight houses, "forming the only approach to anything like a village that we met in the whole country."[11]

In 1948 the Misión Araucana established a school that is taught by a young man, Antonio, eldest son of Segundo Huenchual (Fig. 9, No. 2). The teacher claims to have a gross enrollment of fifty pupils, with an average attendance of thirty nine.[12] One room of a utility building next to Segundo Huenchual's dwelling serves as the sole classroom.

At Renaco the hockey field and the ritual ground are distinct (see Fig. 9). There is no resident *machi* at present, although it was claimed that a male *machi* named José Teuque once lived on the reservation. Despite the presence of a ceremonial area, no *ñillatun* has been held at Renaco for more than ten years.

[11] Smith, 1855, p. 285.

[12] This figure may well be too high. See footnote 7 of this chapter.

SOCIAL STRUCTURE OF RENACO

Renaco's population distribution conforms closely to the pattern described for Cautinche and Carrarriñe. There are fifty-six people grouped into nine households, an average of slightly over six to a dwelling. The number of adults of each sex and the proportion of adults to children may be seen in Table VI.

There are several unusual household combinations in Renaco. House No. 4, for instance, contains a bachelor, his unmarried

TABLE VI

Distribution of Renaco's Population

House No.	Adult Men	Adult Women	Children	Total
1	1	1	4	6
2	1	1	6	8
3	1	1	5	7
4	1	1	2	4
5	3	1	2	6
6	3	3	1	7
7	2	2	2	6
8	1	1	3	5
9	2	3	2	7
Totals	15	14	27	56

sister, and a young brother and sister. Informants said of this householder, Domingo Huenchual, that "he did not wish to marry." A male *machi*, José Teuque, used to occupy structure No. 5, but long ago he moved to Argentina. The house now shelters Francisco Villegas with his wife, two children, and two bachelor brothers. In No. 6 there lives a couple with one small child, two unmarried grown sons, and two unwed adult daughters. Of the four children belonging to the couple in No. 7, one is a bachelor and one a spinster.

Only a single case of polygyny was noted at Renaco. The chief, who lives in No. 1 with one wife, has a second wife in No.

9. Here she resides with a married son and his wife, a bachelor son, an unwed granddaughter, and two small grandchildren. All the women married to Renaco men come from outside reservations, but two brothers from houses Nos. 8 and 9 selected wives from the same place. Like Carrarriñe, Renaco has a fairly high number of unmarried adults of both sexes.

A SOCIOLOGICAL RECONSTRUCTION

When one reviews all the evidence supplied by informants with respect to the origins of the three reservations studied in this chapter, one finds a great many varied data among which a fairly consistent pattern may be detected. It is impossible to reconcile all the disagreements of time and circumstance noted, but if one selects some of the relevant statements that were made, a reasonably clear hypothesis can be put together. Without further apology, the following reconstruction is tentatively offered.

About 1800 a band of Araucanians settled at Nacimiento, near the Bío Bío River. Among them were members of the Painemal, Collío, Nahuelhual, and Huenchual families, all of whom were presumably patrilineally related. The group split about 1825, with the Nahuelhual-Huenchual segment moving to Renaco, while the Collío-Painemal people moved to Carrarriñe. In keeping with cross-cousin marriage rules, the younger Collío-Painemal men married daughters of their Renaco maternal uncles. During those years the Mapuche were not only at war with outsiders but they also seem to have had many internal quarrels, which spurred some of them to detach themselves from established communities and to seek new homes in virgin territory. One instance of this sort took place about 1850, when a dissentient from Carrarriñe, Antío Paineo, left his natal region and founded a new community at Cautinche. Thus, Mapuche settlements seem to have split off from one another by a process somewhat analogous to mitosis. An original "parent cell" at Nacimiento divided into the "daughter cells" of Renaco and Carrarriñe about 1825; and approximately a generation later Carrarriñe divided to form Cautinche. The offspring groups became politically, spatially, and economically detached from the parental settlements, but they established sociological links with one another through the agency of cross-cousin marriage.

To venture just one step further into the realm of hypothesis, there is something in the social composition of the reductions that makes them appear like patrilocal units which are dispersed into a number of multilocal residences. If one imagines a vast roof extending over the entire limits of a reservation, each of them could be viewed as an old-fashioned patrilocal, unilocal residence. In other words, a small reduction, such as Cautinche or Renaco, probably contains much the same association of individuals as would have made up the traditional *loñko's* household and following; and a large reservation like Carrariñe comprises an aggregation of several such households. In some ways the dynamic process by which new Araucanian communities were formed resembles the kind of segmentation which has been discussed elsewhere in connection with the Hopi and other societies.[13]

Great, indeed, is the contrast between the theoretical organization based on the unilocal practices of the past and the actual state of affairs in the present. Each married man usually lives in his own dwelling, which averages six occupants. Few ties hold together the coresidents of a reservation, and divisive tendencies may be noted on each reduction. Relations between communities likewise tend to be slight, but complete isolation is prevented through contacts brought about primarily by reservation exogamy, school attendance at near-by reductions, and participation in *ñillatuns* and the large assemblies known as *kawiñ* or *trawun*.

[13] Titiev, 1944, pp. 46–48; 1943, pp. 522–30.

THE LIFE CYCLE. I. BIRTH TO ADOLESCENCE

PREGNANCY CUSTOMS

As is frequently the case in primitive patrilineal societies, Mapuche wives are anxious to bear offspring, and boys are particularly desired. There is no failure to associate pregnancy with sexual intercourse, but supernatural agents may be invoked to help bring about fertilization. On rare occasions an elderly woman, presumably past childbearing, claims to have become pregnant without copulation. In such cases she attributes her condition to a vision, *perimontu*, in which a fantastic and supposedly supernatural beast possessed her. If her child is born alive, it is allowed to die for fear that it will develop into a monster. J. M. Collío, who told me of this belief, went on to say that a young woman would be laughed at if she claimed to have become pregnant without having had sexual relations.

Barren women consult a female shaman, *machi*, who specializes in such matters. Treatment usually includes drinking the blood of a sacrificed sheep or other animal and swallowing a concoction made from a plant called *wakachu* ("maize grass").[1] Sterility is regarded as incurable if the *machi* decides that it is witch caused, in which case, in Collío's words, "there is nothing to be done but to allow the husband to take another woman."

In some instances a woman who is eager to have a son, whether or not she is already pregnant, may wear the silver figure of a warrior, *aukafe wentru adentu* ("war-man-image"), attached to her breast ornament, *trapelakucha*. In other cases such a woman may suck a little milk from the breast of a relative who is nursing a male child, or else she may seek permission to eat from the same dish with a man who has recently become the father of a son.

In a general sense babies are supposed to come from the sky,

[1] *Wakachu* may also be known as *walumraki*, which Augusta (1916, I: 244) identified as *Paspalum vaginatum* Sw.; family Gramineae.

wenumapu ("high land"). This is also one of the regions to which go the spirits of the dead, but no explicit connection is made between the two sets of ideas. It is the moon which, because of its supposed control of catamenia, is looked upon as the special god of children. When she wants a woman to become pregnant, she causes her menses to stop.[2] There is also a belief in an amorphous spirit of fertility, *choyülchefe*, which controls germination and reproduction in all living things. Together with a feminine counterpart, *choyülchefe* is supposed to dwell in bodies of water such as springs, pools, or cataracts. He is also associated with bees, which return in force each season when germination reaches a peak. *Choyülchefe* is not represented in any concrete form and is not the object of prayers for fertility.

An ambivalent attitude exists toward sexual relations during menstruation. Such relations are forbidden on the grounds that both parties will be subject to disease; yet intercourse at these times, it is thought, will very likely result in impregnation. There is also a belief that women who regularly enjoy orgasms are more likely to have offspring.

Although children are usually greatly desired, there are special situations wherein pregnant women prefer to have abortions. Most frequently these cases involve unwed girls whose lovers refuse to marry them. If enough hard feeling has been aroused, such a girl may resort to a *machi*. The *machi* gives her a strong infusion of cinnamon bark, the bark of the *pucha* tree,[3] and a plant called *tropa* or *trupa*,[4] which is commonly known as devil's tobacco, and which was, in point of fact, formerly smoked by the Araucanians. If this potion proves too strong for the patient, she is given an antidote of *chillko* ("fuchsia"), and a kind of ginger (Spanish, *maqui;* Mapuche,

[2] Cf. Latcham, 1924, p. 626. Latcham, 1909, p. 347, described the moon as the wife of the sun.

[3] The Spanish term is *patagua*, which Augusta (1916, I: 172), identified as *Myrceugenia pitra* Berg, family Myrtaceae.

[4] Identified by Augusta (*op. cit.*, pp. 236–37) as *Lobelia tupa* L., family Campanulaceae.

kul·on). Abortions are rarely sought, however, even among unmarried women, and are ordinarily performed only in conjunction with an act of witchcraft known as *koftun*, the aim of which is to render a worthless lover impotent or sterile.

I was told of no current pregnancy tabus, but Cooper stated: "It was taboo for an expectant mother to stand on the threshold of the hut";[5] and Guevara said that pregnant women were not allowed to visit the sick, watch hockey games or races, or partake of certain foods lest they bear twins.[6] All sources agree that intercourse is not forbidden during the period of gestation.

If a mother of small youngsters finds herself with child, she is likely to prepare them for the coming event by saying that a bird appeared to her in a dream and promised to send the family a new baby for a playmate. She then asks the children to be good to the infant when it arrives. Conventionally, Araucanian children are supposed to be ignorant of the circumstances pertaining to childbirth, and they are not permitted to be present when a birth takes place.

PARTURITION

Unlike the custom of earlier days,[7] a contemporary mother is expected to bear her children within her own *ruka*, and some of the more sophisticated women even go to maternity hospitals in the cities. The process of childbearing is called *choyüin*. On the reservations when the time for delivery draws near, a section of the house is set apart, and no one may come there except those who are assigned to help the patient. Young children are particularly forbidden to approach or touch their mothers, and it is the common practice for all housemates who are not assisting with the case to absent themselves as soon as labor begins.

A parturient woman is usually attended by a midwife or a

[5] Cooper, 1946, p. 732.

[6] Guevara, 1911, p. 285.

[7] There is a sharp contrast between the childbirth customs reported by informants in 1948 and the harsh picture drawn in Latcham, 1909, pp. 359–60.

machi, her own husband, and, occasionally, one other man or woman. She is given a sturdy stick and encouraged to hold it and to walk up and down as long as she can. During labor she takes draughts of water, sometimes mixed with ginger. When parturition is about to occur, the mother assumes a kneeling position on a sheepskin mat large enough to catch whatever matter may be discharged incidental to birth. If help is needed a strong man or woman may grasp the patient and press down on her abdomen. It is thought that particular care must be taken with women having their first babies to make sure that the child is guided through the proper orifice.

As soon as birth has taken place the attendant midwife or *machi* heats a special instrument, *katrüf dowe* ("umbilical cord cutter"), made of sharp metal, formerly of stone. With this instrument, which is reserved for this one use, she severs the cord, then ties the knot. Upon the expulsion of the afterbirth the husband is directed to gather up the sheepskin on which accouchement occurred, and to be sure that it contains every particle of solid and fluid substance that was shed at the confinement. Should anything have fallen to the ground, the husband carefully scrapes it up and puts it into the sheepskin. The mat and its contents are then secretly buried in a deep hole, dug in virgin soil at an unfrequented spot. A stone or a heavy piece of wood may be used as a weight to prevent animals from getting at the buried bundle. Secrecy is observed for fear of witches or of jealous people, such as lovers or women who may want the recently delivered mother for a daughter-in-law.

Soon after a delivery has been safely accomplished, all soiled garments and bedding are carefully laundered in a stream. Mother and child are bathed in a mixture of water and the fragrant leaves of plants such as *foye*,[8] *ifulkoñ*,[9] or *natruñ*.[10] Sometimes, if a daughter has just been born, the mother may

[8] *Foye* is the cinnamon tree which is called *canelo* in Spanish. It is very sacred to the Araucanians and is used in a wide range of religious contexts.

[9] Augusta (1916, I: 65) identified this plant as *Vestia lycioides*.

[10] Identified as *Solanum Gayanum* Remy, family Solaneaceae, in Augusta (*op. cit.*, p. 146).

be given a strong and bitter drink made from the leaves either of the *foye* or *fol·o*.[11] The idea seems to be that the beverage is so powerful that it will strengthen the woman and enable her to bear a son next time.

In a sense the Araucanians consider that a newly born infant is on trial; that is, before devoting themselves to it wholeheartedly, they want some assurance that it is sound enough to survive. As a combination test of weakness and remedy for it the baby may be given a drink of cold water, mixed with the juice of the *refu* plant.[12] A belief prevails that this drink will either make the child stronger by cleansing its stomach and forcing it to urinate, or cause it to die; but my informant admitted that he had never heard of an infant that had actually perished from the treatment. Sometimes, too, parents perform a little rite designed to give strength to a child. Early in the morning after a night when the moon is full, they hold the baby over the fire in their own home. The father takes the feet, and the mother holds the head. Gently they stretch the infant, praying that it may grow and be strong.

A lying-in period that may extend to ten days or two weeks follows confinement. When the mother feels herself fully recovered, she takes a bath in water made fragrant with the leaves of aromatic plants. Not until a woman has thus announced her recovery are her other young offspring free to see her and the baby at close range. For immature children to approach their recently delivered mother too soon is thought to be dangerous, causing boys to be weaklings and girls to be so enfeebled that they will die in childbirth when their time comes. No set date is fixed for the resumption of marital relations. Each couple makes its own arrangements after the wife feels that she has returned to normal health and activity.[13]

[11] *Fol·o* is identified in Augusta (*op. cit.*, p. 50) as *Boldoa fragrans*. Whisky or cognac is sometimes substituted nowadays for the native beverage.

[12] Augusta (*op. cit.*, p. 51) failed to identify *refu*, but described it as a short shrub with yellow flowers and small round leaves.

[13] Latcham (1909, p. 360) said that cohabitation is not resumed until a child "has cut all its teeth." Cooper (1946, p. 733) mentioned abstinence

INFANCY

Babies are encouraged to nurse as soon as possible. If a mother's milk fails or proves unsuited, as judged from the appearance of a child's skin, tongue, or excreta, any friendly lactating woman may be called upon for help. Sometimes, a group of helpers may work in shifts, with one nursing a child early in the morning, another in the forenoon, a third at noon, and so on. Sometimes, too, in polygynous households, comates may help to suckle each other's young. "No how," exclaimed Collío in one of his interviews, "will they let a baby starve!" One Araucanian man told me that he had been suckled, at least in part, by the wife of his oldest paternal uncle; a paternal grandmother helped with the nursing of another. Such evidence confirms the importance of the household unit as a basic, functional group of kindred, for each of these wet nurses, through the agency of unilocal, patrilocal residence, was a housemate of the child she helped to suckle.

The concept that the first few days of an infant's life constitute a kind of trial period also finds expression in the naming customs. No discussion of a name takes place before a baby is at least a week old and has given indication that it is in good health and will probably live. The option of naming a first child customarily belongs to the paternal grandparents, but if they have many descendants they may, out of courtesy, transfer the privilege to the mother's parents. Either the grandfather or grandmother, depending on the sex of the infant, serves as godparent, holding the babe in his arms, and giving it his own name before witnesses.[14] So closely is the custom followed that the term *l·aku*, father's father, also means namesake, and the naming rite is called *l·akutun*.[15] If he can afford it, a godparent gives presents to a namesake. Traditionally, the gifts

for as much as a year or eighteen months. Very likely, the abandonment of polygyny has led to an earlier resumption of sexual relations.

[14] A variant account of naming practices occurs in Housse, 1939, pp. 255 ff.

[15] *L'aku* is a reciprocal term for a man's father's father and son's son, and *chuchu* or *llalla* refers to a woman's mother's mother or daughter's daughter (Figs. 2, 3). Augusta (1916, I: 109) gave namesake as one of the meanings of *l·aku*.

consist of baby animals of the child's own sex. Thus a boy may receive a male colt, calf, or lamb. These are herded with the family's livestock until the child is old enough to look after them himself.

For children other than the first any relative or neighbor (neighbors are likely to be relatives), may act as name giver. Anyone who wants to serve in this capacity may ask if an infant has yet been named. If it has not, he has only to hold the child and announce its name, usually the same as his own, before witnesses. In cases of this sort, the bestowal of gifts is entirely optional, and the godparent incurs no obligation whatsoever.

Formerly, an infant spent the first year or so of its life strapped in a cradleboard, *kupulwe*, but the custom is no longer universal. The Araucanian cradleboard (Pl. II, Fig. 2) is made with a sort of visor to protect the child from the sun, for too much sunlight is believed to cause freckling and cross-eyes. A child is swaddled in soft cloth and then fastened in place with soft leather thongs, in preference to string or cord. Tiny infants are very rarely left alone. Most often they are carried along by the mother wherever she goes, and the cradleboard is placed beside the mother's bed so that she may attend to the child's needs if it cries at night.

Neither weaning nor toilet training follows a rigid pattern. Parents may exert a little pressure in these matters, but on the whole a small child is allowed to follow its own inclinations. The nursing period does not seem to be unduly prolonged,[16] and while a baby is being weaned, it gradually begins to eat the same foods as adults. As to toilet habits, children are taught to defecate out of doors, but they learn to urinate into a small pottery jar, *metawe*, kept within the *ruka*.[17] Each morning the chamber pot is emptied into a larger pottery vessel, kept out-

[16] No instances of suckling up to the age when all the teeth are cut were observed, although such cases are reported in the literature. See Latcham, 1909, p. 360.

[17] Grown women may continue to use chamber pots indoors, especially when the weather is bad, but men generally go outdoors. At a public ceremony in Malalche a man paused to urinate unashamedly in full view of a large number of spectators.

side, where it is allowed to "ripen" for use as medicine, "soap," or as a mordant. Infant excretions on the dirt floor of a *ruka* are treated with calm indifference. On one occasion I watched a little boy being held by his mother while he vomited into the fireplace. No one, except this observer, seemed greatly concerned.

Although the Araucanians are no longer addicted to bathing in icy streams, as was their ancient custom, mothers still prefer to wash their small youngsters in cold water and to wrap them warmly afterward. Children are bathed often, and the laundering of their clothing is an important feminine occupation. The urine of young boys is highly esteemed for cleaning and shampooing and is said to be particularly good for cleansing the hair of dandruff and vermin. It is rinsed off with water and soap.[18]

When a child is between six and nine months old it is taken from its cradleboard and allowed to crawl on all fours. Soon thereafter it is taught to walk, guided and encouraged by its mother, perhaps with the help of two parallel bamboo rails set at a convenient height.[19]

As is to be expected, Araucanian children suffer from numerous ailments. When a youngster is ill he is kept indoors close by the fire, and his mother gives him such home treatments as she can. If these fail she may call in a more experienced woman, who examines the child and prescribes additional remedies. The term for medicine is *l·awen*, and two of the most popular items are *piukel·awen*[20] ("heart-medicine"), and *liq-l·awen* ("white-medicine"), tentatively identified as quinoa, which is supposed to be good for stomach ailments.

Decoctions of aromatic plants like ginger and cinnamon are

[18] Several informants confirmed the uses of urine as here given. Those who do not have soap may use a saponaceous plant, *kül·a*, identified in Augusta (1916, I: 104) as *Chusquea* spec.

[19] Housse, 1939, p. 255. I was told about this device, but I had no opportunity to see it in use. It is described and pictured in Joseph, 1933, pp. 714–15.

[20] Augusta (1916, I: 185) identified it as *Linum selaginoides* Lam., family Linaceae.

also widely used in curing. A patient who runs a fever is bathed in water tinctured with fragrant leaves, massaged, wrapped in clean clothes, and put to bed. Swellings and inflammation are counteracted by the external application of burnt earth and ashes, taken from the fireplace and compounded with herbs. Similar mixtures are taken internally as a remedy for indigestion. So far as could be discovered, a professional shaman is never called in to treat a sick child under the age of puberty, nor are youngsters ever made the subjects of the elaborate and expensive curing rites known as *machitun*. If an infant dies it is promptly buried without much ceremony and is, apparently, soon forgotten.

Araucanians of today are very fond of their offspring and indulge their desires; they seldom scold or strike them. Only if children are exceptionally troublesome are they sometimes punished by slapping or whipping with a leather strap. Old-fashioned as well as modern child training puts great stress on the inculcation of respect. Children were taught to show respect to all their elders, and more particularly to the fathers of families, especially if they happened to be *loñkos*. Youngsters of either sex who showed disrespect by eating before their elders or by taking things without permission used to be punished by snatching or pinching at their genitals. (Incidentally, gripping a man's testicles, *lolotun*, was a common trick in fighting; and co-wives, *müriwen*, occasionally punished a bad husband in this manner. This was a sanctioned procedure and was not supposed to lead to reprisals.)

Children were also taught not to lie or steal, never to desert their relatives, not to become too intimate with strangers, not to eavesdrop, and never to enter or look into strange houses. They were strongly cautioned against leaving home after dark, and those who disobeyed were told that *ñunechen* ("God") would cut short their lives; or else that an evil spirit, *añchimallen*, would snatch away their shadows (souls).

Until very recently bad little boys or girls were frightened by the sudden appearance of a man wearing a black mask, *koloñ*.[21]

[21] Typical masks are figured in Joseph, 1931*a*, p. 72.

Mapuche masks are simple affairs, usually carved of wood and worn over the face. They always resemble the human face, and never that of an animal or some inanimate object. Sometimes masks are said to represent generalized evil spirits called *wekufü*, but in public ceremonies they may be worn by sanctioned clowns. It used to be customary for each household to have a *koloñ* or two on hand, but this is no more the case, and only a few people still possess masks.

A masker would come to frighten a child by prearrangement with the parents in cases, for example, in which a youngster was known to have the bad habit of wandering out of the house after nightfall. But if a child were unexpectedly troublesome, or had an extended crying spell, any neighboring friend or relative might show up of his own volition.

Frightening a naughty youngster was formerly carried out at two different levels of intensity. In milder cases, when the parents heard a masker coming they would instruct the child to hide in a sack, from which they released him as soon as the wearer of the *koloñ* had departed. If this treatment failed of its effect, a masker would carry off the child in the sack in which it was hidden. He would speak loudly of throwing his bundle into the river or among wild animals, but soon he would pretend to tire and put the sack down, thus giving the child a chance to escape and scamper home.

Nowadays, informal education begins as soon as a child learns to walk and to speak Mapuche. He is taught not to approach the fireplace too closely, never to waste food, and to be honest. During the long nights of the winter season he hears many folk tales that convey moral lessons, tribal legends and beliefs, accounts of military exploits, and cleverly worded songs that cover a wide range of topics.[22] Boys, especially, are encouraged to memorize and sing songs and to learn to speak well and boldly, for oratory and verbal skill are highly regarded masculine accomplishments.

Other aspects of education for small youngsters are left primarily to mothers and womenfolk, since men work in the

[22] Housse, 1939, p. 267; and Titiev, 1949, p. 4.

fields or are away from home much of the time. For the most part, however, children under six or seven years spend their waking hours at play. Little boys run races, wrestle and pull one another's hair, pretend to plow, and walk about carrying miniature hockey sticks with which they strike at a ball or at any small stone or object along the path. Girls prefer to play with dolls fashioned of cane or bamboo into human shape, *puñeñkantu*. They take care of them as if they were babies, dressing and undressing them, and occasionally pretending to hold curing rites over them because they are supposed to be ill.

CHILDHOOD

Before they have reached the seventh birthday youngsters begin to pass out of the carefree stage of infancy, and to learn the tasks that are appropriate to their sex. Sometimes they receive spoken instructions from their elders, but more often they learn from observation and imitation. Adults make it a point to take them along when they leave the house, and to converse with them while they are at work. In this way children are made ready to undertake their first serious chores, which usually consist of herding and caring for sheep. Boys or girls generally serve as shepherds between the ages of six or seven and twelve. They take their flocks out to graze in the morning, and if they expect to remain away until late in the day they may take some bread or parched wheat, plain or sweetened with honey. At some time in the afternoon the herders drive their flocks into a corral or a field near home, and go into the house for the midday meal.

The children have various ways of amusing themselves in order not to be lonesome while they are herding. Most often they sing aloud the songs they have learned from their elders, and occasionally they shout something for other shepherds in the neighborhood to hear. They do not try to carry on actual conversations at long distance, but they get a sense of companionship simply from hearing one another's voices when they are out of sight. This is especially true on misty days, when each little shepherd feels cut off from the rest of the world.

Sometimes, when he is out with his flock, a boy will practice hockey or run dashes by himself. At other times he may straddle a stout piece of bamboo, pretending that it is a horse, and gallop about. He may even heighten the illusion by inserting bits of cloth at one end of the stick to serve as ears, and he may wind thread about one end for use as bridle and reins. Another favorite pastime is to collect bits of sticks and twigs, and to insert them into the ground in patterns that suggest houses, corrals, stables, animals, and similar familiar objects.

Girls may continue to tend sheep for an extended period of years, but boys are impatient to turn the duty over to a younger sibling at the first opportunity. Thereafter, boys begin to go into the fields with the men, and they learn to handle horses and oxen, and to perform agricultural duties. They also begin to take hockey more seriously, and they attend matches played by teams of adults. They race and wrestle more vigorously, and they become skilled in the use of slings and bolas with which they hunt small animals. Their sisters, besides herding sheep, are learning to cook and weave and to run a household. Before long teen-aged boys and girls acquire all the skills of adults and begin to assume the tasks and responsibilities of grown men and women.

Preadolescent brothers and sisters enjoy great familiarity. They joke and play together freely, sing, and tell stories. Occasionally, they test their fortitude, or allow their elders to do so, by burning bits of linseed wood or linseed straw against the skin of hand or arm. This custom, called *kopan*, was once widely in vogue and had a special significance. Every child on the verge of puberty had four marks burned with linseed on the wrist and elbow joints, and these marks were supposed to light his way to the other world if he died. *Kopan* is still commonly practiced. It is looked upon as a test of bravery, for a child who brushes off the bit of glowing coal is branded a coward. It also has the significance of a minor rite of divination, in the belief that no serious injury will result if a youngster is destined to grow into a healthy adult.

ADOLESCENCE

Latcham made repeated references to totemic or tribal initiations, but he gave no details, and it is hard to tell whether he was dealing with a custom that once prevailed or with a hypothesis.[23] Certainly, no practice currently exists that in any way resembles a formal recognition of adulthood. The transition from boyhood to manhood is completely unmarked and gradual and is accomplished as a boy assumes more and more adult tasks and begins to engage in sexual relations.

In the past an adolescent boy was given a pair of severe tests to show his all-round development. At the age of eleven or twelve he was mounted on horseback and sent alone for a visit of several days at the house of a friendly chief. The latter spent much time with him, conversed with and questioned him on a variety of topics, and took mental note of his deportment and replies. Soon after the lad's return home, the chief secretly gave his father a full and critical evaluation of the boy's behavior. About five years later, a youth was expected to give a public demonstration of his oratorical ability and the power of his memory.[24]

Girls, too, are said formerly to have been subjected to an initiation on reaching puberty, and there is a likelihood that the custom persists in areas near the Cordilleras,[25] but in the region in which I worked no mention of such a trait was made. The beginning of a girl's menstrual cycle receives no public mention. On the contrary, unmarried women keep their periods secret from all but their mothers, and wives from all but their husbands. It is even said that women wear no protective pads, although they may place an extra mat in bed, because lack of privacy in a *ruka* would betray their condition. Garments or bedclothes that absorb the discharge are promptly laundered with exceptional care. Unwillingness to reveal the menarche, to resort to menstrual huts, or to wear protective pads, stems

[23] Latcham, 1924, p. 467, *et passim.*

[24] Housse, 1939, pp. 261 ff.

[25] *Ibid.*, p. 257.

not from indifference but rather from the fear that a woman can be easily bewitched if an enemy gets hold of some of the discharge.

There is a simple folk tale that is supposed to explain the origin of catamenia. A long time ago, a young woman went out in the dark to urinate against the slope of a hill. Just then the moon rose and saw her vagina. The moon regarded this as a lack of respect and punished her by causing her to menstruate every twenty eight days. The term for menstruation is *peküyen·n*, "caught by the moon," *küyen·*, and the phases of the moon are figuratively likened to a woman's life cycle. Thus, a new moon is a virgin, a full moon a pregnant female, and a waning moon is a sterile old woman.[26] The close connection thought to exist between the moon and fertility helps to explain why intercourse with a menstruant is supposed to be likely to cause pregnancy.

[26] Cf. Latcham, 1924, p. 626.

THE LIFE CYCLE. II. ADOLESCENCE TO DEATH

PREMARITAL SEX CUSTOMS[1]

WHEN a youth achieves adulthood, he is given much advice by older men. He is cautioned not to overindulge in sexual activity, but he is by no means urged to remain celibate until married. Young women, similarly, are taught not to offer themselves too freely, but they are not told to cherish virginity, except in the case of Christian families. Masturbation is said to be indulged in by boys, but, although some informants felt that the practice is increasing, all agreed that it is not widespread. Homosexuality is reported to be moderately common among young girls in the spring. According to a typical native opinion expressed during a discussion, these habits indicate that such youngsters are ready to be married. Berdaches, pederasts, and sodomists are not infrequently mentioned in the literature, particularly in conjunction with shamanism;[2] but little was said or known about these practices at present. One informant did volunteer the statement that sodomy with ewes was becoming fairly common, and he attributed its origin to the Argentine, where, he claimed, the act was performed with female llamas. On the whole sodomy is considered dangerous and likely to cause disease, but bachelors observed in the act are simply advised to get married.

A girl with a high mound of Venus is considered particularly attractive. It is conventional for men to seek out and choose as mistresses or wives such girls as they find desirable, but women are not supposed to take the initiative in selecting lovers. When a man finds an opportunity for intercourse he acts promptly. There is no anticipatory fondling or "petting" and not much time is devoted to preliminaries.[3] Consummation

[1] This section comprises material obtained from several informants, of whom the principal one was J. M. Collío.

[2] Latcham, 1924, p. 629–30.

[3] One old-time polygynist, who had observed the conventional politeness and deference of Euro-American males, expressed wonder that they ever succeeded in gaining possession of a woman.

takes place in the conventional position, and the male reaches a climax without thought of bringing his partner to an orgasm, even if he is aware of this aspect of feminine physiology. There is no record of the use of contraceptives and, except for married couples, intercourse generally takes place outdoors. Some care is taken to achieve privacy, but little shame or guilt attends discovery, except in cases of adultery.

Trouble is likely to result from love affairs, primarily because men regard them as ends in themselves, whereas women tend to consider them as preludes to marriage. Lovers take advantage of this attitude to promise marriage to any girl they court, but these promises are repeatedly broken. Not much can be done in such an event unless the girl becomes pregnant. She may then seek help from her lover's mother and, if the latter wants her as a daughter-in-law, she may urge her son to marry. If a pregnant girl finds herself repudiated by her sweetheart she may, in extreme cases, commit suicide, or else she may seek vengeance by asking a *machi* to perform the *koftun*.[4] *Koftun* is designed to render the guilty man impotent or sterile, but it requires the sacrifice of the baby which is either aborted or strangled at birth by the *machi*. The infant's ovaries or testicles are cut out and slowly burnt, while the *machi* dances about the fire, praying that the offender may become emasculated.

Koftun may also be performed against a girl who refuses to marry her lover. Revenge may then be taken by his mother who, by one device or another, gets some of the girl's menstrual blood. She dries it and either inserts it into the victim's food, or puts it into a fire to be consumed. In either event the girl is supposed to sicken, die, or lose her sexual powers.

Mr. Donaldson knew of instances in which a couple lived together before marrying as a kind of fertility test. In cases of this sort, marriage is supposed to follow as soon as pregnancy has occurred. Here again, some men fail to live up to their promises and brazenly refuse to marry or they go to Argentina.

[4] Cf. Augusta, 1916, I: 91; and Cooper, 1946, p. 733.

A bastard, *weda fine* ("bad" or "wasted semen"), is usually reared by the mother's parents. Two types of illegitimate offspring are recognized. One kind, born to a promiscuous woman, is called *kiñe ñuke mari chau* ("one-mother-ten-father"). The other sort, whose father is almost certainly known, is termed *yall tuku*, which signifies "made without love." Girls who have borne bastards are not regarded as unfit or ineligible for marriage. If later a suitor seeks to make an issue of such an occurrence, people hasten to say, "Oh, that was a long time ago," or else, "It wasn't her fault. She was forced into it."

Early writers have drawn word pictures of unrestrained license among the Araucanians, particularly at festivals where there has been much drinking.[5] There may be some truth to such assertions, but at least one Mapuche informant insisted that it is not easy to have a love affair during big assemblies because there are so many people present and all watch one another.

Prostitution has been reported, and Latcham has even said that some harlots travel "from village to village in pursuit of new lovers."[6] It is hard to explain the presence of such an institution or custom in a society that affords so many opportunities for sexual indulgence to people of either sex. It may be that the term "prostitution" has been used more or less figuratively as a synonym for unchastity, but I was unable to verify the occurrence of actual venality. The nearest approach to harlotry about which my informants spoke was furnished by a class of widows who, having made up their minds that they are unlikely to rewed, freely invite the youths of the neighborhood to disport with them. That such women expect payment for their favors is highly doubtful.

There seems to be a growing tendency for young men to resort to brothels in the Chilean towns and cities which they have occasion to visit. This is associated, in the expressed opinions of informants, with the breakdown of the traditional social

[5] Latcham, 1909, pp. 354, 356, 367, 370; 1924, p. 629. On the other hand, one author has made the surprising statement that "*entre los araucanos no se conoce el adulterio*." Treutler, 1861, p. 70.

[6] Latcham, 1909, p. 354.

structure. Specifically, they attribute the habit of consorting with prostitutes to the greater individual freedom and lack of supervision brought about by private ownership of land and neolocal residence, as well as to the new opportunities for acquiring money through the sale of one's goods or services. Very likely, too, the rising frequency of visits to bawdy houses may be a by-product of the sociocultural forces that have brought about increasing numbers of bachelors.

COURTSHIP PRACTICES

So long as the custom of unilateral cross-cousin marriage was the universal rule, courtship behavior was restricted and standardized. When a young man was ready to marry, he talked with his elders, an eligible girl was selected, and the youth's *loñko* supervised negotiations with the *loñko*, parents, and other household mates of the prospective bride. Since the disintegration of the old system, more varied forms of courtship have come into being. Some of these, including premarital sexual relations, have already been discussed.

If a young man resides on a large reservation that contains several families which are not closely related, he may court a local girl while she is fetching water, or whenever she passes by a field where he is at work. In small reductions, in which all the inhabitants are likely to be close kin, a boy may have to contrive a suitable opportunity to woo a girl from another place. This he may bring about by making an extended visit to a relative or friend, by taking a job away from home, or by attending public assemblies at various reservations. Under other circumstances occasions for courtship arise when young men and women meet in government schools or during social functions sponsored by missionaries.

Nowadays, it sometimes happens that a young couple reach an agreement to marry without consulting their parents and without setting an exact date. When such an understanding prevails an impatient lover is likely to seek access to his sweetheart by employing the services of a go-between who is intimately familiar with all the domestic arrangements of the girl's household. With the aid of the pander, who must be able to keep the dogs quiet and under control, the young man enters his sweetheart's home in the night and crawls into her bed. This custom of sleeping together is called *inakudun*. Nothing much is made of it if it is plainly preliminary to marriage, but a girl who gets the reputation of freely sharing her bed becomes a laughing stock and is known as *uñam domo* ("loose woman").

MARRIAGE[7]

When, in the course of time, a man decides to marry he is not expected to deal directly with the girl or her parents. Instead, he is supposed to employ a friendly couple to serve as go-between. The process of arranging a nuptial pact is *dakeltun*, and the intermediaries are termed *dakelchefe*. The latter hold lengthy conversations with the prospective groom and his parents, during which they carefully memorize the exact wording of the marriage offer, with particular reference to the details of a proposed bride price. After that the *dakelchefe* make a long stay at the girl's home, where they ingratiate themselves with her family and await a favorable chance to present the groom's proposal. During this period the female go-between constantly accompanies the bride-to-be, helping her to dress and to carry out her daily chores. She also seizes every occasion to praise the suitor and to paint a glowing picture of connubial bliss.

If all goes well and preliminary assent has been won to the suggested arrangements, the *dakelchefe* return to the groom's house to render a complete account of everything that was said and done during the visit. Thereafter, the boy's father schedules an assembly, *trawun*, to which is invited a large gathering including the bride and her relatives. As the festiv-

[7] While discussing this topic informants did not always differentiate clearly between present-day usages and traditional customs, but the intent of this section is to portray the contemporary situation. Compare the treatment of marriage in Moesbach, 1930, pp. 231–69; and Cooper, 1946, pp. 719–20.

ities proceed people seat themselves on skins or blankets, food and drinks are served, and elderly men and women may smoke pipes. Soon joking, *ayükulen*, begins and, as the crowd warms up, songs are rendered by anyone who desires to sing.[8] No matter who else sings, a chance is always provided for the suitor to make a proposal, which the intended bride is expected to parry.[9] "*C'est de bon ton*," as Housse expressed it.[10] Nevertheless, before the assembly breaks up, the groom's father gives a valuable present to the girl's father as a token of the bride price, and the couple contrive to set a date for an "abduction."[11]

When the appointed time comes the groom sets out on horseback after dark, accompanied by a small party comprising brothers, male cousins, or friends. The bride and her family may or may not offer a spirited resistance, but in any event the lover manages to seize his sweetheart and to ride off with her to the home of an intermediary, *rañiñelwe*, where, by previous arrangement, the couple spend the night. The next morning, in the presence of witnesses, the *rañiñelwe* notifies the groom's father that his son has abducted a woman, and the father publicly announces the extent of the payment he is prepared to make to the girl's father. Arrangements are then completed for the *ñillanentun*, which is the bestowal of the purchase price. This step is also taken before witnesses to discourage either party from violating earlier agreements. When, at last, the entire transaction has been completed, a go-between brings the fathers of the principals together so that they may shake hands in public. At this stage the girl's parents bring household goods and other presents for the newlyweds, and the bride's mother is expected to invite the couple and her daughter's affinal relatives to pay a visit to her home. From this time on,

[8] This custom is described in Titiev, 1949.

[9] *Ibid.*, p. 13.

[10] Housse, 1939, p. 242.

[11] Reference is here made to the Araucanian custom generally called "mock rape." The Mapuche consistently describe the custom by the Spanish word *rapto*, which may be translated either as "rape" or "abduction."

the respective mothers-in-law may refer to each other as *ñillandomo*, which signifies "women united through the payment of a bride price."

The Araucanian custom of "mock rape" or abduction has for years aroused the interest of social scientists. No single explanation can possibly cover all the variations of the practice, which has differed at various stages of Mapuche history and which fluctuates with a man's wealth and previous marital experience. For example, marriage by abduction is customarily the rule only for the first of a man's wives, and today the institution is kept alive primarily by rich men of high prestige. Other marriages center about an exchange of gifts, and natives point out that neither party expects to gain very much in these transactions. Any profit will probably be spent in mutual entertainment.

In times past abduction seems to have taken place in at least three different contexts. When they were fighting intratribal wars, Araucanian men sometimes raided enemy settlements and literally carried away women whose resistance was anything but simulated. In other cases men abducted brides without prearrangement, but later made adequate payment; and in many instances the entire affair was worked out in advance, and resistance was purely formal.

After reviewing all the pertinent data, it may be concluded that out and out abduction of women was a rare phenomenon that was occasionally brought about by a combination of exogamy and a continuous state of internal warfare. Much more commonly, abduction and its concomitant resistance seem to imply only a highly dramatic form of "ceremonial coyness." As I have elsewhere written: "'Ceremonial coyness' is best explained by the reluctance one feels at leaving a familiar home to take up residence in a strange one, especially if one's new family is to be merged with that of the parents-in-law."[12] The applicability of this interpretation to the Araucanians has been indicated in an analysis of social singing wherein it was pointed out:

[12] Titiev, 1943, p. 517, footnote 30.

It is the postmarital residence pattern that appears to put the greatest strain on a newlywed woman. While a groom continues to live on his natal reducción, sometimes in the very house in which he was born, a bride must go to live among strangers in a strange place. Not only must she work out an adjustment to her husband, but also to such of his relatives as happen to live under the same roof. Some of the personality clashes that are likely to grow out of this situation are revealed in 'Woman's Song' Nos. 5, 6, 7, and 9.[13]

Further proof that the Araucanians themselves recognize how difficult a strain unilocal, patrilocal residence imposes on a bride may be found in the customs of postmarital oratory and visiting. Soon after a daughter has been "abducted," as was noted above, her parents come to stay at her new home for several days during which they receive the bride price, present gifts, and extend invitations for return visits. While the wedding festivities are still in progress, the bride's father addresses a long speech to his son-in-law, urging him to have no fear, asking him to treat his wife fairly and considerately, and offering to take back his daughter if ever the groom should tire of her. The groom's father also gives advice to the newlyweds. Somewhat later the couple pays a return visit to the bride's natal home. There is much feasting and talking and many questions are asked to determine how the young wife is getting along. Quite commonly, plans for future visits are made at this time.

Despite the strains and stresses brought about by the marriage customs divorces, as distinct from mere separations, rarely occur. A woman who is unhappily married may, indeed, insist on returning to her natal home and having the bride price restored to the groom. Unless such action is taken very soon after a marriage, however, it is apt to lead to so much unpleasantness that it is avoided. In fact, distressed brides sometimes prefer suicide to any other arrangement.[14] The rarity of divorce is also correlated with the practice of polygyny, for a dissatisfied husband may take another mate without the need of divorcing his previous spouse. If he finds that the two women cannot get

[13] Titiev, 1949, p. 16.

[14] Cf. Housse, 1939, p. 240.

along in one household, he may build a separate *ruka* for the discarded wife. The latter could insist on returning to her parents, but if she is the mother of grown children who can attend to her wants, she may prefer living in her own establishment to going back to her natal home.

Married women are expected to be faithful to their mates, but no serious restrictions are placed on the postmarital conduct of men. Although an adulterous wife is supposedly subject to any punishment her husband cares to inflict on her,[15] it is doubtful if men often carry out severe reprisals. In the great majority of cases married couples learn to make whatever adjustments are necessary and to live out their lives while making the best of any situation that confronts them.

DEATH AND FUNERAL CUSTOMS[16]

Ignorance of sanitation and medical care, combined with inadequate housing and improper diets, prevent many Araucanians from living to a ripe old age. As soon as a person dies word is sent out to his neighbors and to friends and relatives living on other reservations. Only minor differences occur in the burial patterns for adults of either sex; even funerals of suicides do not depart from customary lines. More elaborate ceremonies and richer grave offerings may accompany the rites of prominent and weathly persons, but the general procedure is much the same for all.

When a person dies his housemates wash the body, arrange the hair, and dress the deceased in his best clothes. The corpse is usually kept indoors for three or four days, during which the section of the *ruka* in which it lies is tabu to small children. If the person had a favorite hockey stick, musical instrument, or household utensil, it is kept beside the body, but the rest of his possessions may be freely handled and soon pass into normal use among his heirs. There is little fear of contact with a corpse. Even the bedding on which a dying person lay is washed and again utilized, except when wealthy people prefer to give it

[15] Latcham, 1909, p. 354.

[16] Cf. the accounts in Guevara, 1908, pp. 263–84; 1929, II: 33–56; and Housse, 1939, pp. 217–21.

away, or when fear of a contagious disease makes it seem wiser to burn the bedclothes.

Formerly it was a common practice to call in a *machi* or some special practitioner to perform a kind of autopsy in order to determine the cause of death.[17] Although this custom is no longer widespread, a simple rite of divination still prevails. As soon as death has taken place, two dishes of parched wheat, carefully smoothed over, are put at either side of the head. Before sunrise next morning they are closely examined. If they show impressions of feet, or if the corpse's head has inclined sharply to one side or the other, it is supposed to mean that another death will soon occur in the neighborhood.

Burial is delayed for several days so that all who have been notified of the event may gather at the home of the deceased. Meanwhile, there is much feasting and drinking, with symbolic participation by the corpse. Preparations for interment are made as soon as relatives and friends have had time to assemble. The body is enclosed either in a conventional coffin or in an old-fashioned "canoe" made by bisecting a stout tree trunk lengthwise. Each half is then hollowed out, the body is put into the lower half, and the upper segment is fitted over it and tied on as a lid. Food, wine, tools, and offerings contributed by friends and acquaintances are placed inside.

On the day of the funeral the coffin and all associated gear are placed outdoors. Two pairs of orators, known as *weupins*, representing the dead person's matrilineal and patrilineal connections, then deliver lengthy eulogies, during which they recite the life story of the departed one, call to mind his ancestry, dwell on his fine character, and make public his expressed wishes for the disposal of his property. There is much wailing by relatives, sometimes augmented by professional mourners. Araucanian men as well as women are expected to grieve by weeping, and mournful blasts are emitted on the *trutruka*.

[17] According to Edwards (1929, p. 49) the personage who performs this office is called *cupolave,* but Smith (1855, p. 236) stated that *machis* make autopsies. A lengthy account of such a ceremony that took place in 1892 is given in Latcham (1909, pp. 365–70).

Shortly before a burial takes place severel young men from the reduction dig a grave in the local cemetery. On such occasions a reservation functions as a group of kin. There are no professional gravediggers, and those who volunteer their services are subjected to no tabus. The Araucanians prefer spacious cemeteries, completely enclosed and entered through a single gate which can be locked (see Pl. X, Fig. 2). Orientation is generally to the west, and members of both sexes may be buried side by side, but one section is usually set apart for children. Mention was made of burial plots reserved for the use of groups of relatives, but the nature of such groups could not be ascertained.[18] A variety of grave types may be found in a single cemetery. For instance, at Malalche, near Cautinche, there were four kinds of graves within one enclosure. They were: old style, with the body encased in two halves of a thick tree trunk; a newer kind, in which the corpse rests in a coffin and the plot is enclosed by a small picket fence; children's graves, marked only with small individual crosses; and the grave of a *machi*, distinguished by her *rewe* set at its foot and also marked with a large wooden cross and surrounded by a picket fence (Pl. X, Fig. 1).

A corpse may be conveyed to the cemetery in an oxcart, but more often it is likely to be carried on a sort of stretcher borne by men. There is a convention that when a body is being thus carried it must not be set down between the house and the place of burial. Should it happen to touch the ground en route, a cross must be erected to mark the spot.[19] Since much drunkenness prevails at funerals, it is said that some corpses are repeatedly tumbled to earth. Housse stated that mounted men charge ahead as if to induce a spirit to follow them and, con-

[18] Cf. Cooper (1946, p. 735), who said: "Each family or lineage had its own burial ground near the dwelling . . . to which the body was carried. . . on a stretcher or in the coffin." At Cautinche one of the cemeteries is close to the spot where the first house was built, and another is near a new settlement made in 1917. See Figure 4, near houses Nos. 16 and 1, and Plate X, Figure 2.

[19] Wooden crosses are also placed wherever a murder occurred or a body has been found.

versely, that ashes are spread on the way home to prevent the soul's return.[20] I was unable to verify these practices.

Interment takes place in a deep grave. *Mudai* or *chicha* is poured into the opening, and other offerings may be added. At one time it seems to have been the custom to kill a man's favorite horse over his grave and to bury it in an adjacent plot, but this is no longer done.[21] According to Housse, the more grave offerings a person receives, the better his soul's fate in the afterlife.[22] So strong a hold does this notion have that even Christian Indians are often observed putting objects, more or less surreptitiously, into the graves of their dead.

After the deposit of food, drink, and other gifts, the grave is filled in and covered with a heavy log. It was explained that this is done to protect the body from inclement weather, to keep out wild animals, and to prevent witches from snatching the remains for conversion into a *witranalwe*. At the close of the rites the grave is carefully smoothed, and four days later members of the bereaved family thoroughly inspect the surface for signs of disturbance. More offerings are sometimes made on these occasions, after which the grave is no longer visited, except by those who observe Christian customs. There is no evidence of a native belief in the periodic return of spirits of the dead.

OTHER-WORLD NOTIONS

Araucanian notions of souls and spirits are seldom given overt expression, but many of their beliefs are indirectly stated. There are numerous variations of their basic concepts, but in general they believe in multiple souls,[23] and they have a tendency to equate a number of spirit-containing factors including

[20] Housse, 1939, p. 219. Also, see Guevara, 1908, pp. 263–84. Detailed accounts of the traditional rites for a chief may be found in Moesbach, 1930, pp. 395–415, and in Joseph, 1933, pp. 515–26.

[21] Lothrop wrote me that at La Serena llamas used to be sacrificed.

[22] Housse, 1939, p. 89.

[23] Cooper (1946, p. 735) said: "There is no clear evidence in our original sources that the Mapuche-Huilliche believed men to have two or more 'souls.'" Among contemporary Araucanians there is widespread belief in multiple souls as the phrase is customarily used in anthropological literature. On this point see Latcham, 1924, pp. 579–86.

heart, saliva, shadow, reflection, and picture. They fear, for instance, that there is danger of losing the soul if one spits in the house of a stranger, who may turn out to be a witch, and they are reluctant to reveal their names or to have their pictures taken.[24]

When death occurs the vital spirit or soul, *am*, becomes separated from the body, leaving the corpse inanimate and inarticulate. Yet the body is somehow supposed to remain aware of what is going on about it. Hence, speeches are addressed to it, food is offered, and it may be entrusted with messages to kinfolk who died long ago. Furthermore, the Mapuche do not hurry to bury their dead, especially bodies of influential persons, as they feel it possible to maintain contact with the soul while the deceased is in the house. This explains why it was formerly the rule to smoke the cadavers of important personages and to retain their bodies within the home for as long as a year.[25] Once burial has taken place, however, the soul is supposed to go to the other world; it continues to play a part on earth as long as the deceased is actively remembered, especially if he is the subject of dreams. With the passage of time, when people no longer think, talk, or dream of a departed person, his death comes to be regarded as final.

There are many divergent accounts of the fate of a soul after death and burial. Most often it is said that the spirits of the dead go to *kütralmapu* ("fireland"), a place associated with the sun; but some say that disembodied souls go to a place above the earth, *wenumapu;* or underground, *minchemapu;* or across the sea, *n·omel·afken*, or *karkul·afken*. I could arrive at no clear idea of the distinctions among these various other worlds, nor could I discover what class of souls go to each place, except in the case of witches whose spirits go to the cave or *renü* with which they were formerly associated.[26]

[24] Cf. Smith, 1855, p. 222.

[25] Cf. Cooper, 1946, p. 735. Lothrop called attention to the fact that the bodies of Inca rulers were long held in houses and that corpses were "smoked" in Panama.

[26] Housse (1939, pp. 88–90) said that ordinary souls cross the Pacific or disappear in the setting sun, whereas chiefs become birds or flies, warriors

While it is universally agreed that the souls of the dead continue to exist in the afterworld, the manner of existence is variously and only vaguely described. As a rule, the belief prevails that men and women carry on shadowy replicas of their lives on earth, following the same pursuits, raising the same crops, marrying, and having children.[27] Informants were unable to say whether spirits die in the other world, but it was explicitly stated that the souls of the dead are not reborn on earth in the bodies of babies. Departed spirits are considered capable of exerting some influence on the living, especially through the agency of dreams. If they are displeased by their funeral services, or if they are manipulated by witches, spirits can wreak harm on mankind, but no systematic rites of propitiation are carried out.

---

live on in clouds, and witches are chained in active volcanoes. Compare Cooper, 1946, pp. 736–37.

[27] Molina (1808, p. 81) made a similar statement: "The soul, when separated from the body, exercises in another life the same functions that it performed in this, with no other difference except that they are unaccompanied with fatigue or satiety." See also Latcham, 1924, pp. 580–81.

WITCHCRAFT AND CURING PRACTICES

Belief in witchcraft, ever widespread among the Araucanians, is still a pervasive element of their culture.[1] A witch or sorcerer, *kal·ku*, seldom operates individually, but is usually thought to be in league with others of his kind. Each *kal·ku* is supposed to train a youngster in the ways of sorcery, but the novice is sworn to secrecy and seldom practices witchery until he is old. Aged women are particularly apt to be suspected of witchcraft. By native definition, a *kal·ku* is one who deliberately harms or kills a person, generally upon request and payment by an enemy of the victim or else because of jealousy. A witch may or may not be related to the injured party, but he who employs a sorcerer must be prepared, if the victim succumbs, to have one of his own kinfolk die to even the score. In this sense, resort to witchcraft is regarded as a gamble.

A suspected witch was formerly tried before a *loñko* and an assembly of his followers. If the testimony of at least two witnesses or accusers was accepted, the sorcerer was supposed to be slain on the day of the victim's funeral.[2] According to one of the accounts I was given, based on stories a thirty-eight-year-old informant had heard in youth, a guilty witch was tied and dragged by a man on horseback from her home to a spot where a blazing fire had been kindled. She was then beheaded, but to prevent any artful recovery, she was cut into pieces and these were thrown into the fire to be burnt to ashes. If a chief did not want to inflict such severe punishment, he could have the accused witch driven off his territory. Together with her close relatives she would thus be forced to wander from place to place until she found a *loñko* who was willing to accept her and her party. Such a chief might be a distant kinsman, an old friend,

[1] Practically every source dealing with Araucanian culture contains some material on witchcraft and curing. Particularly full accounts that supplement this field report are readily available in Latcham, 1909, pp. 350–53; 1924, pp. 770–822, *et passim;* and Métraux, 1939.

[2] Cf. Molina, 1808, p. 78; and Smith, 1855, p. 237.

a broad-minded or kindly individual, or a leader who was willing to take a chance in order to augment his following.

Nowadays, for fear of retaliation, witches are neither killed nor driven away, but they may be induced to leave voluntarily by means of intensive whispering campaigns, or because their neighbors obviously shun them. In fact, it is part of the education of children to warn them to have nothing to do with people suspected of witchcraft. There is reason to believe that some of the Chilean Araucanians who go to Argentina are people under suspicion of being sorcerers.

WITCHCRAFT ACTIVITIES

Witches' sabbaths are supposed to be observed in underground caverns or *renüs*. Almost all caves or depressions in the earth are likely to be regarded as *renüs*, wherein dwell all manner of dangerous beasts whom the sorcerers use as familiars. Greatly feared in this context are a wide range of animals including lizards, snakes, foxes, butterflies, partridges, dogs, rats, and, particularly, any creatures of unfamiliar appearance, monsters, or freaks such as two-headed calves. The cries of many birds, or the appearance of animals that unexpectedly cross one's path, are widely held to be portents of sickness and death. So deep-seated is the fear of unusual animals, that some Araucanians who visit the zoological gardens in Santiago come away convinced that the keepers and, by extension, all Chileans must be powerful witches.

Sorcerers exercise their power by controlling evil spirits, the entire class of which may be termed *wekufü*.[3] *Wekufü* occur in many guises, especially in the shapes of the aforementioned beasts and monsters, but they may also take other forms. Conspicuous among these are *piwichen*, a terrifying vampire, sight or sound of which is a sure portent of death, and *choñchoñ*, which is described as a human head equipped with wings. To see or hear it while it is in flight portends death. Whether

[3] Latcham (1909, pp. 351 ff.) distinguished between *huecuvus* ("evil spirits") and *huecuvuyes* ("sorcerers"). He also set up separate categories for *dunguve* ("diviner") and *machi* ("witch doctor" or "exorcist").

witches can directly control the actions of *piwichen* or *choñchoñ* is a moot question among the people, but all are agreed that these creatures are somehow implicated in sorcery. One popular tale will suffice to illustrate a number of witchcraft beliefs. It concerns a man who was courting a girl that lived at some distance from his home. Whenever he went to see her he would hear the call of a *choñchoñ* and begin to feel violently ill. His elders advised him that the next time this happened he should plunge his knife into the ground. He followed their instructions and, to his surprise, a winged head fell to earth. He thought that it resembled his mistress, so he hurried to her house and there he found her headless body lying on its back. Thereupon, he deliberately rolled the body over, to prevent the head from reattaching itself properly. Then he went home, and the very next day he received word that his sweetheart had died.

A common cluster of witchcraft practices revolves about the use of various things associated with heat and light. They are known collectively as *cherufe*, a word applied to a miscellaneous category that includes stones supposedly derived from the sun or active volcanoes, meteorites and aerolites, comets, shooting stars, and will-o-the-wisps. All witches are believed to own *cherufes*, particularly in the shape of oddly formed stones taken from flaming volcanoes. These particular *cherufes* are sometimes winged, and fly at the command of sorcerers to consume a victim's blood and make him subject to tuberculosis, pneumonia, or some other serious ailment.

Two other classes of *wekufü*, frequently involved in the exercise of sorcery, are *witranalwe* and *añchimallen*. These terms signify two kinds of corpses stolen from graveyards and put to evil service by powerful witches. A *witranalwe* is made from the body of an adult and corresponds somewhat to our popular idea of a ghost. It is white, and its outline may be seen but never its face. Ordinarily, a *witranalwe* goes about only by night, on horseback. Its favorite trick is to bedevil and mislead any person traveling after dark, and to meet a *witranalwe* is a sure omen of disaster, sickness, or death. Exciting encounters with *witranalwe* and narrow escapes from them are favorite subjects of stories, and such beliefs explain why parents fear to permit children to wander out of the house after dark. If an object is lost or inexplicably moved from one place to another, a *witranalwe* is held to blame.

Añchimallen is similar to *witranalwe*, except that it originates from the corpse of a child. In addition to being small an *añchimallen* can only go afoot, which means that its range of travel is greatly restricted. People say that an *añchimallen* may sometimes be glimpsed as a will-o-the-wisp.[4]

Despite the prevalence of such beliefs, it is important to note that the spirits of the dead are not looked upon as harmful and are not feared unless witches convert them into *witranalwes* or *añchimallens*.

Most common of all the activities for which sorcerers are held directly responsible are those causing sickness and death. Like many primitive people, the Araucanians are unwilling to accept death as natural, but attribute all deaths to witchcraft. Latcham thinks that an exception is made for those dying of wounds received while fighting,[5] but that all other kinds of violent or accidental deaths are thought to be somehow engineered or brought about by the agency of sorcerers.

Two types of irregular behavior or insanity are differentiated by some of the Mapuche. One kind, *wesa loñko* ("bad head"), refers to any sort of extravagant conduct, such as that of a person who is extremely lewd. The other kind, lunacy or paranoia, is termed *wedwed*, and is usually held to be caused by witches.

When an enemy wants to have some one bewitched, the most common procedure is to furnish a *kal·ku* with a bit of matter (for example, feces, saliva, hair, or saliva-moistened food) which was once intimately connected with the body of the intended victim. Menstrual blood, fresh or dried, is particularly potent, especially if the supply is built up over a period of several months. For this reason girls are warned to be very wary

[4] Further details on these topics may be obtained from Guevara, 1898, pp. 222 ff.; Latcham, 1924, pp. 770–823; and Métraux, 1939, pp. 329–32.

[5] Latcham, 1924, p. 741.

of accepting help in the laundering of stained garments. If the substance furnished is moist, the witch secures it firmly with vegetable fibres and places it in a *renü*. If the material is dry it is cast into a fire. In either event, the victim is supposed to grow thin, sicken, and die, as the substance dries out or is consumed.

Another technique involves the use of similar materials which the sorcerer contrives to introduce into an unsuspecting victim's food. Should a client fail to procure the usual body stuff employed, a witch may prepare a poison, *funapue*, made from the body of a type of lizard known as *fillkuñ*. Those who consume such poisons are supposed to die within six months.[6]

An interesting example of contemporary sorcery practices was related by the Reverend Harry Donaldson. About 1931, while he was living at the home of Juan Antinao in Cautinche, a *machi* made repeated efforts to kill him.[7] For her first attempt she butchered a sheep stolen from Antinao's flock, performed some rites over it, smeared some of its blood on several coins and notes, and scattered them in conspicuous places. Mr. Donaldson picked them up and spread them through the community while purchasing supplies. When no harm befell him, the *machi* left some of the slain beast's flesh on Mr. Donaldson's doorstep, and he fed it to the dogs. After a time the *machi* announced that Christian power was stronger than hers and desisted from further efforts.

BELIEFS REGARDING SICKNESS

One of the most interesting aspects of Mr. Donaldson's narrative is the fact that witchcraft was attempted by a *machi*. Ethnological literature contains many instances of a close correspondence between sorcerer and shaman, but on the whole Araucanians do not equate *kal·ku* and *machi*. They recognize

[6] Widespread belief in poisoning through sorcery explains why the Araucanians perform autopsies to determine the cause of death.

[7] It was a *machi* who was using her supernatural power to perform sorcery. Since *machis* are the religious leaders of the Mapuche they are violently opposed to Christian clergymen.

that both deal with supernatural forces, and they freely express the opinion that each knows much of the other's lore, but whereas *kal·kus* are shunned and feared, *machis* are called upon for help. Quite often, as a matter of fact, a *machi* may be asked to counteract the work of a sorcerer; and *machis* are even thought to have the power to enter a *renü* in order to remove whatever substance a witch may be drying out. Just the same, some say with a knowing chuckle, it is best not to arouse a *machi* because if she gets angry, or if her fees are not paid, she may work hand in hand with a witch, or she herself may engage in sorcery.

Apparently, the Araucanians believe in a sort of dualism in which good powers that sustain society oppose evil forces that disrupt the social order. These notions are never unequivocally expressed, for the Mapuche do not systematize their religious beliefs, but two forms of evidence can be cited in support of a dualistic interpretation. For one thing, the natives speak of beneficent deities, *kümeñunechen*, who oppose spirits of evil, known as *wesañunechen*. The latter operate through witches and *wekufü* to cause illness and death, and the former function to oppose them through the agency of *machis*. Equally important is evidence based on a sort of origin myth. Long, long ago, runs the story, a mythical serpent, *kaikai*, raised a flood to overwhelm mankind, but it was counteracted by a magic mountain, *treñtreñ*, that rose ever higher to provide refuge for enough living things to repopulate the earth.[8] The struggle between the two sets of forces is never-ending. Evil powers continue to plague mankind with ailments brought about by *piwichen*, *choñchoñ*, *cherufe*, *witranalwe*, or *añchimallen*. Against them strive the *machis* with the help of prophetic dreams sent by well-disposed supernatural agents.[9]

[8] For further details of this myth see Oyarzún, 1917; and Soustelle, 1938, pp. 39–43.

[9] A *machi* who has dreamed in the night must sing and beat her drum on the next day. Probably, they have frequent dreams, for one or the other of Carrarriñe's two *machis* could be heard beating her drum on numerous occasions.

CURING RITES

When a grown person falls ill his housemates try to treat him to the best of their ability. If he grows much worse, conferences are held among his adult male relatives and, if they feel that the case is sufficiently serious, they may decide to undertake the trouble and expense of calling for the services of a *machi*. Once this decision is reached, a delegation goes to visit the *machi*, taking along some of the patient's undergarments and a sample of feces or urine. From her examination of these things the *machi* diagnoses the ailment. Another form of diagnosis consists of the transfer of disease-laden saliva from a patient to an animal. Later, the *machi* kills the beast and studies its organs to determine the cause and nature of the sickness.[10] If she thinks that the illness is serious but that she can effect a cure, she will agree to perform the lengthy curing rite called *machitun*.[11] For this purpose, the patient is sometimes transported to the *machi*'s home, or else the *machi*, with her assistants and paraphernalia, may come to the sick person's house.

In anticipation of the *machi*'s arrival, approximately twenty people, a few women but more men, assemble at the home of the patient. Branches of cinnamon are set in the ground at his head and feet, and the *machi* undresses and examines him carefully. She, or her assistant, beats the shaman drum, *kul·truñ*, shakes rattles, sings, and prays. From time to time, at the conclusion of a verse or at some other appropriate interval, the *machi* orders the bystanders to raise the conventional shout, *yapen* or *kefafan*, which is supposed to frighten away evil spirits. Ten or twelve men generally serve as a kind of chorus. They hold hockey sticks or lengths of bamboo, and at the *machi*'s command they clash their sticks over the sick person's body and shout, "Ya, ya, YAI!" After a while, the *machi* bathes the pa-

[10] Housse, 1939, p. 225.

[11] For comparative descriptions of *machituns* consult Guevara, 1929, II: 114–40; Moesbach, 1930, pp. 350–70; Métraux, 1939, pp. 340–48; and Housse, 1939, pp. 232 ff. A variety of *machi* songs are given in Augusta, 1934, pp. 303–21.

tient, massages his body with fragrant leaves, sucks out, *fochañ*, whatever infection she discovers (or pretends to find), gives him a drink of herbs, and prepares to divine the exact cause and nature of his ailment and the cure for it. This is the great climax of the *machitun*. By way of preparation the shaman drinks copiously of ripened urine, *fai willeñ*, mixed with a solution of ginger and cinnamon, and gives some to her helpers. She then sings and beats the *kul·truñ* more and more vigorously, jumps over the patient from one side to the other, and works herself up to such a pitch that she is supposed to go out of her mind and become possessed, *küimin*. Thereupon, she begins to speak with the voice of the spirit that has possessed her but never does she reveal the name of her familiar.

At this stage another person engages her in conversation. He is an experienced and trustworthy man, who was previously selected for the task. He is called *duñumachife* ("interlocutor" or "interpreter"), and he must be a good speaker and endowed with a powerful memory. This man asks many leading questions of the entranced *machi*, cleverly urging her to tell as much as possible about the case, and remembering exactly what she says. After a time the *machi* stops talking and begins a violent dance. Very often she suddenly rushes out of the house to climb up and down her *rewe*.[12] She then dances around the pole, accompanied by a sturdy young man whose special function it is to catch her when she finally collapses and to hold her tightly until she returns to normal. *Machis* are said to select as special assistants men whose embrace will give them pleasure.

Members of the patient's household now provide the *machi* with water so that she may wash and restore herself. When she is ready, the *duñumachife* relates verbatim all that was said while she was possessed. The *machi* pays careful heed, explains the meaning of her remarks, tells what she has learned from the spirit's statements, and prescribes such remedies and treatment as she considers necessary. This concludes the *ma-*

[12] If a *machi* cures at home she uses her own *rewe*, but if she works at the patient's house, she generally orders a duplicate post to be erected in his yard.

chitun, after which the assemblage enjoys a hearty feast. Soon after, the *machi* returns home, accompanied by the same delegation that first sought her services. Part of her payment, which may consist of produce, jewelry, animals, and implements, is made at once, and the remainder is given at a stipulated date, often with the addition of numerous gifts. A *machi* must be paid in full, whether or not the patient recovers. Deaths are blamed on evil spirits beyond the *machi*'s control.

All *machituns* are conducted along the pattern just described. Many variations exist, however, because each *machi* has full charge of a ceremony and must be immediately obeyed by all participants. Individual whims may thus enter into the conduct of the rites. Then, too, certain differences arise from the natures of the various ailments that are being cured. Not all *machis* profess to be equally skilled in handling every kind of illness. Specialization in particular diseases is common. As one skeptic pointed out, this has the practical value of limiting competition. Molina long ago classified curers as *ampives*, who work with herbs; *vileus*, who extract insects; and *machis* who counteract witch-caused diseases.[13]

MACHI PERSONALITY

Considerable variation exists among the personalities of those who become *machis*. Many years ago the office was generally held by men, and it is practically certain that they were abnormal, at least with respect to sexual conduct. Some of them may have been true hermaphrodites, the rest were berdaches or transvestites, and widespread indulgence in sodomy and pederasty was common.[14] There then followed a period when the post of *machi* might be filled by a man or a woman,[15] and at this stage sexual irregularity is less frequently charged, particularly in regard to female practitioners. At present, male *machis* are rare, and some sexual irregularity is still associated with them (Pl. IX, Fig. 1). Certainly, they wear feminine clothes while performing their duties, and it is not unlikely

[13] Molina, 1808, II: 91.

[14] Latcham, 1924, p. 630. Medicine men are described in Smith, 1855, pp. 234–36. Also, see Moesbach, 1930, pp. 330–49.

[15] Cf. Housse, 1939, p. 113.

that they are homosexuals. For all that, their services are much in demand, and many natives regard them as more efficient than are women. Nevertheless, the great majority of contemporary *machis* are women who seem to be sexually normal.[16] They marry, bear children, care for their households, and follow the usual feminine occupations, except when engaged in professional activities. A suggestion of homosexuality is revealed in their relations with novices and assistants, and whispers of adultery during *machituns* are not uncommon, but the older pattern of marked sexual abnormality no longer prevails.

The person who becomes a *machi* must have a strong will and character, partly because of the danger implied in the close conceptual link of witch and shaman, and partly because of the long and arduous training program. Many young women deliberately avoid all *machis*, and so difficult has it become to secure recruits that established practitioners may resort to subtle threats in order to get newcomers to join their ranks. If they meet a likely girl who is the descendant of a former *machi*, they may tell her that she is going to sicken and die unless she takes up the profession. More commonly, especially if a young, single woman becomes a patient, a *machi* may tell her that she cannot recover unless she agrees to serve as an apprentice after her cure. Coercion is not necessarily employed in all cases. Some women voluntarily apply for training, presumably because of the high fees they may earn. Another class of recruits includes people who have had narrow escapes from death by lightning. There is a belief that sometimes a frightened woman faints during a severe thunderstorm and finds on recovery that she has acquired the knowledge and power to be a *machi*.[17] If she decides to accept the call, she is supposed to be superior to an ordinary curer.

[16] Compare the independently made summary of the transition from male to female *machis* in Cooper, 1946, p. 750.

[17] Cf. Cooper (1946, p. 750): "A person took the profession not by free choice or quest; the calling was rather imposed supernaturally upon her."

TRAINING A NEW MACHI

When, in one way or another, a young woman decides to become a *machi*, she offers her services to an experienced and well-known practitioner. Since every highly regarded *machi* has need for one or two assistants, arrangements are usually readily made. The novice goes to live with her tutor for a period of a year or more, during which they work and sleep together. Whether or not they actually enjoy homosexual relations is uncertain. From her tutor the acolyte learns how to diagnose ailments, how to identify medicinal plants, what preparations to make in curing various diseases, how to play the *kul·truñ* and shake gourd rattles, how to communicate with spirits by singing, praying, and dancing, and finally, how to become possessed and to speak with the voice of a spirit. As she acquires these accomplishments the neophyte assists her tutor at *machituns* and *ñillatuns*, and when she has mastered all the required lore, she prepares to give a public demonstration of her skill. This professional debut is known as *machiluwn*, and at its completion the novice emerges as a full-fledged *machi*, ready to practice in her own right.

The *machiluwn* centers about the dedication of a new *rewe*. Attention has already been called to the fact that the *rewe* is the visible sign of a practicing *machi*. It is a stout post or tree trunk, with several steps cut into one side, and it culminates at the top in a small, flat platform. Every active *machi* has a *rewe* planted in the ground before her house. It is set at an angle, and cinnamon and other branches are usually affixed to the upper end (Pl. VII, Fig. 2). Occasionally, a *rewe* has the semblance of a face carved above the last step (Pl. X, Fig. 1). At her death, a *machi*'s *rewe* is brought to the cemetery and placed at the foot of her grave (Pl. X, Fig. 1). When a novice is ready to commence her own career, her male relatives prepare a *rewe* for her, and her tutor sets a date and invites guests to observe the ceremony accompanying its erection.

To some extent the procedure of a *machiluwn* follows the

pattern of a *machitun*, with the neophyte in the role of patient.[18] As the rites progress the older *machi* rubs the body of her pupil with a highly polished black stone, supposedly a *cherufe*. At one stage, too, both parties cut their fingers deeply and mingle their blood by clasping hands.[19] Later, the candidate acts, for the last time, in the capacity of assistant to her tutor. On this occasion the helper is allowed to use a new *kul·truñ*, made for her by a husband or male kinsman and decorated according to the teacher's instructions.[20] As in the case of curing performances, the *machi* becomes possessed and speaks with the voice of a spirit to an interlocutor. At this time the novice may also become entranced, but she is not yet permitted to talk. Soon, both principals ascend the *rewe*, dance around it, and collapse in the arms of their respective masculine helpers. Feasting follows their recovery, after which the experienced *machi* goes home, the guests depart, and the new *machi* is ready to accept her first professional case.

REDEDICATION CEREMONIES

Every year, at the fiesta of San Juan, which in southern latitudes is near the time of the winter solstice, each active *machi* is supposed to rededicate herself and her *rewe* at a celebration termed *ñeikurewen*.[21] The affair takes place at her home, to which numerous guests are invited. Much food and drink, as well as a sacrificial lamb, must be provided by the hostess.

Guests arrive on the evening before the main events take

[18] Many additional details are given in Robles, 1912, pp. 155–70, and in Métraux, 1939, pp. 319–29. According to Robles several *machis* co-operate to initiate a novice. Among other things they "cure" the candidate by sucking parts of her body till they are raw and bloody.

[19] Housse, 1939, p. 101.

[20] Typical markings on a *kul·truñ* are shown in Plate VIII.

[21] A sexual or marital relationship is indicated by the term *ñeikurewen*, as *kurewen* means a wedded pair, and *kuretun* means copulation. Through the rededication rites the *machi* is supposed to be remarried to her *rewe*. It may be that *ñeikurewen* also applies, as was suggested by Edwards (1930, p. 29), to a new *machi's* first consecration of a *rewe*, in which she symbolically marries a *canelo* or other sacred tree.

place. At twilight they surround the *rewe*, while the *machi* sings and prays to the good spirits that act as her familiars. Food is then served and the assemblage retires for the night. Early in the morning lengthy prayers are recited, and a lamb is sacrificed. Some of the blood is daubed on the *machi*'s cheeks, the rest is offered to the good spirits, and the flesh is cooked and served in a sort of communion breakfast. There follows a program of prayers, songs, and dances, to the accompaniment of *trutrukas*, *llollkins*, *kul·truñs*, and *pifullkas*. At intervals the *machi* climbs her *rewe* to engage in solitary prayer (see Pl. VIII). As the afternoon progresses the *rewe* is redecorated with sprigs of cinnamon and ginger, and the celebration concludes with a hearty feast.[22] It is widely held that a *machi*'s power will fail and her following diminish unless she is willing to go to the trouble and expense of holding an annual *ñeikurewen*. Apart from this function and the staging of *machituns*, a *machi* is expected to dream and play her *kul·truñ*, to conduct the *ñillatun* rites described in the next chapter, to interpret dreams and omens, and to pray for victory during important hockey matches.[23]

[22] Although I was not privileged to attend a *ñeikurewen*, I could hear the songs and shouts raised at a celebration while I was living in Carrarriñe. On the next day I purposely walked past the *machi's* house and saw her freshly decorated *rewe*, to which a small Chilean flag had been affixed.

[23] Cf. Cooper, 1946, pp. 750–51.

ASSEMBLIES, GAMES, AND CEREMONIES

ASSEMBLIES

LARGE assemblies known as *kawiñ* or *trawun* are important features of Araucanian culture.[1] Their impact on the lives of the people can best be appreciated in the light of certain aspects of their social organization. It must be recalled that Mapuche communities are characterized by an absence of physical cohesion and a corresponding lack of communal activities. Throughout the year there is a fair amount of intrareservation visiting, but contacts with other reductions are quite rare, especially in the cold and rainy season when roads wash out and travel is all but impossible. For several months of each year, therefore, every settlement tends to be cut off from its neighbors:

> The virtual isolation that prevails in winter is relieved in the spring and fall when intergroup gatherings . . . are held. Members of a given reservation act as hosts, and guests are invited from other districts. Various motives may serve to bring about these meetings. They may be held for the purpose of reaching policy decisions that affect all the participants,[2] to honor a person returning from Argentina or some other distant place,[3] to celebrate a holiday . . . or simply for the sake of friendship and sociability. Whatever their particular aims may be, all such assemblies are welcome events that provide opportunities for friendly conversation, courtship, gossip, and the exchange of news. Regardless of special functions, too, these events always include in the schedule of activities feasting, drinking, oratory, and singing.[4]

Notwithstanding the variety of purposes underlying these reunions, they seem to follow a similar pattern, and even the

[1] These words may be variously spelled, and some writers try to distinguish between them on the basis of function. All public assemblies have so many points in common that it seems permissible to treat them together. Cf. Robles, 1912, p. 171.

[2] McBride (1936, p. 311) described a congress held to discuss land problems.

[3] A meeting of this sort is reported in Robles, 1912, pp. 171–81.

[4] Titiev, 1949, pp. 3–4.

events that are avowedly secular are interspersed with prayers and other forms of religious expression. One of the most important assemblies, held annually on Saint John's Day, even points to the existence of a kind of ritual calendar. The use of Saint John's Day is not necessarily an instance of basic Christian influence. Even the most pagan of the Mapuche use the term because it is a convenient way of designating the winter solstice, which almost coincides with the fiesta of San Juan on June 24. To most Araucanians Saint John's Day marks the coming of spring and the start of a new year. In their own language the date is known as *rañiñtripantu* ("mid-point of the year") or *wetripantu* ("new year").[5] The following account of a San Juan fiesta is based on material supplied by Domingo Carilaf, school teacher at Carrarriñe, who got it from his grandmother.

With the approach of the year's turning point each *loñko* or cacique would send his *werkens* to invite a large number of guests. Customarily, these included married daughters with their children, husbands and affinal relatives, as well as other kinfolk and personal friends. The chief's retainers would prepare great amounts of favorite foods and beverages, and the guests were expected to bring much bread and freshly slaughtered meat, but no beverages. Just prior to the arrival of the visitors, the *loñko* sacrificed a sheep and prayed for peace and happiness for himself, his followers, and his guests. While praying he would look up to the sky, addressing himself to the good deity *ñunechen*, often called *chau* ("father"). From time to time he would blow on the *pimuntuwe*, a perforated stone disc, which the Mapuche regarded with great reverence;[6] and every now and then he would sprinkle from a wooden dish some of the sacrificed sheep's blood.

Guests were expected to remain from two to seven days.

[5] Augusta (1916, I: 233) gave an excellent rendering of the meanings of *wetripantu: "El tiempo en que vuelve el sol del norte (año nuevo según el cómputo natural), la primavera; el año neuvo (político).*" See also Augusta, 1934, p. 35; and Cooper, 1946, p. 747.

[6] *Pimuntuwes* are pictured and discussed in Joseph, 1931*a*, pp. 36–38.

Each was cordially greeted, and usually responded with a gift. Ordinary folk sat on skins or woven mats, but chiefs were seated on piles of soft things that formed a kind of sofa. Each day lengthy conversations were held among the head men, during which they reviewed their family histories, checked over their respective genealogies, questioned one another about the status of their families, caught up on vital statistics, and discussed the general state of affairs of their people. When a morning's talk was ended there was feasting and drinking,[7] followed by singing and dancing,[8] often to the accompaniment of native musical instruments. Although these assemblies included religious activities, they were presided over only by lay chiefs, and not by *machis*.[9]

Since the collapse of the older social structure, large reunions are no longer regularly scheduled to celebrate the new year. They continue to be held in modified form, owing to the disappearance of functional chiefs, on occasions such as weddings, funerals, visits of married daughters to their natal reservations, and *ñillatuns*.

GAMES

"Perhaps the most important single recreational activity of the Mapuche-Huilliche," wrote Cooper, "was the *kawiñ*".[10] Contained within the complex of the great assemblies was indulgence in numerous games and sports, but these might also be played apart from reunions. Araucanian games were of two

[7] Cooper (1946, p. 739) wrote: "The *kawiñ* was very apt to end in widespread intoxication among the participants, bloody fights, and sex orgies—in a word, the typical, widely distributed aboriginal South American drinking bout."

[8] Latcham (1924, p. 502) spoke of a dance called *lonco meu*, which may mean either dance of the headman or chief or dance of head movements. The former is more generally termed *loñko purun*. Latcham said that *lonco meu* was performed as a greeting and welcome to a visiting cacique, which fits the context of the San Juan fiesta. For additional details, consult Manquilef, 1914, pp. 167 ff.

[9] Latcham (1924, p. 503, *et passim*) tended to view the assemblies made up essentially of kinfolk as totemic affairs.

[10] Cooper, 1946, p. 738.

major sorts, athletic events and gambling competitions. For the latter the Mapuche used beans painted black on one side, sticks, playing cards of hide, and marked bits of bone or wood comparable to dice.[11] In addition, there was much wagering on the results of athletic contests. Among their favorite sports were wrestling, swimming, foot racing, lance play, a kind of volley ball, *pillma*, and most important of all, hockey.

Araucanian hockey (Spanish, *chueca;* Mapuche, *palikantun*) was once regarded as the conditioning sport par excellence for warriors, and is still the principal and universal game played by men.[12] So thoroughly intertwined were the concepts of war and hockey, that in speaking of a *loñko*'s followers more than one informant used terms for warrior and hockey player interchangeably. Such great importance was attached to the matches that each side performed rituals to bring about victory, players had to observe sex tabus before important games, and heavy bets were placed on the results. Also, as has been indicated hockey sticks are clashed to drive away spirits of evil during ceremonies, and we shall find that hockey plays a part in the great *ñillatun* celebrations.

Chueca, as it is most commonly called, is closely comparable to field hockey. It is played on a long, rectangular field, about 300 or 350 feet long and forty feet wide, the limits of which are marked by a line or light furrow made with a bullock-drawn plow. Each man uses a homemade hockey stick three to four feet long, fashioned of hard wood, rubbed smooth, and curved at one end.[13] The ball, which is somewhat smaller than a billiard ball, is made of wood and is sometimes wrapped tightly with wool thread or bound in leather. Each team consists of ten to twelve players, but the number may be larger or smaller by mutual consent. Rules are quite simple. When the contest

[11] Smith (1855, pp. 320–23) and Manquilef (1914, pp. 105 ff.) have supplied many added details.

[12] Cooper (1946, p. 739) said that men, women, and children played hockey; but I could find no evidence of participation by adult females, although young girls and boys did play together.

[13] For a lengthy description of hockey and its significance, see Manquilef, 1914, pp. 140 ff.

starts, the ball is placed in a slight depression exactly at mid-field. The opposing centers face each other with sticks crossed over the ball, and at a shouted signal of "Ya!" each tries to hit the ball toward the opponent's goal. Thereafter, the progress of the game consists of trying to drive the ball over the end of the field defended by the enemy without letting it cross either side line. Defenders, of course, strive to prevent this, chiefly by forcing the ball outside the playing area. As soon as the ball goes out of bounds play stops, and the game commences again with a new face-off at mid-field. There is little organized team play, and little specialization of functions (Pl. XV, Fig. 2). Once the ball is in play, everyone shifts from offense to defense as the situation demands. No one is especially designated to guard goal, and when a long hit is made everyone runs after the ball, the offensive team trying to keep it in bounds until it crosses the goal line, and the defensive side struggling to knock it out of bounds. Blocking and tripping are permitted, and there is no such thing as illegal use of hands, but no point is scored if the ball is kicked or thrown across the goal line. Whenever the ball is improperly handled, or if a man is badly hurt, play is stopped and a face-off takes place in the center of the field.

Every little boy, in ancient times, was given a stick and taught to play. Under the supervision of an older man, often a *loñko*, youngsters were organized into teams and encouraged to compete. As they grew older they formed groups, each of which had its own captain. To summon his team the captain sounded his *kullkull*, the Araucanian equivalent of an army bugle, which was formerly used also to assemble warriors or to sound warning of an enemy raid.

When *chueca* was played avowedly as a training exercise for war, games lasted for long periods of time, because neither team could win unless the score was four to zero. Each goal made by an opponent cancelled a point for the other side, somewhat on the order of deuce in tennis. Hence it often happened that two teams struggled for the better part of a day before either side won.

Not many changes have been introduced into the contemporary version of *chueca*. It is still the favorite sport of men, and good players are held in esteem. No longer, however, can men devote themselves as completely to sports as was once the case. Because of the pressure of farming duties, hockey games are seldom played except in the late fall, between the end of the summer harvest and the maturing of the winter crops. The "little summer of Saint John" is a good season for games and Sunday is a favorite day. In communities where Christian influence is strong games are often played after services. No longer, too, are matches allowed to last indefinitely. By agreement contests are generally limited to stipulated time periods, as, for example, two 30-minute halves, between which players rest and change sides. All goals count one point, and the team which has the higher score is the winner.

Nowadays, players select their own captain,[14] usually picking the best man of the group, who serves as center. Around the center are clustered the fleetest runners and strongest competitors, while the less skillful are spread toward the goals. Substitutions are permitted if a player tires or is hurt. Older men and boys watch from the side lines and shout encouragement to their favorite team. Spectators usually carry their hockey sticks along, with which they gleefully return the ball when it goes out of bounds. Once in a while a number of elderly men and boys are permitted to join teams of young adults, either for fun or for practice. Matches are most commonly played between factions of the same reservation, but more excitement and betting occur in games between picked teams from two reductions. A contest of this sort, representing a sort of championship event, takes place annually in Cholchol in conjunction with Chile's Independence Day on September 18. On this occasion, I was told, rival *machis* hold ceremonies to help their sides win, and during the progress of a match they pronounce spells to call the ball across the opposing goal line.[15]

[14] There is a possibility that *loñkos* formerly selected team captains.

[15] Examples of hockey songs may be found in Augusta, 1934, pp. 332–34.

There is a possibility that rituals accompany important inter-reservation games, but no rites are performed for local events.

An opportunity to witness a good contest came on the afternoon of Sunday, June 27, 1948. The weather was clear and the sound of a *kullkull* indicated that there was to be a match on Carrarriñe's main field (See Pl. XI, Fig. 2).[16] When we arrived at the spot we found that there were eight players on each team, representing supporters of two of Carrarriñe's three schools. Fifty to sixty young and old men stood on the side lines and cheered lustily, if informally. Formations and organized plays were at a minimum, except that a player sometimes blocked one or more opponents in order to give a teammate a chance to strike the ball. As this field has a marked slope, sides were changed from time to time. Nothing serious was at stake, and although the men played hard and fast, there was little roughness, and good-natured banter was exchanged between opponents and between players and bystanders.

ÑILLATUN CEREMONIES[17]

Woven together into the great composite of *ñillatun* rites are elements of *machi* lore, assembly customs, hockey games, curing and divination practices, and numerous other religious features, all of which are mingled in a two-day public celebration that is designed to give thanks for favors received or to ask for help in times of stress. This greatest of Araucanian ceremonies is singularly hard to define in precise terms. Above all, one cannot determine the names or characteristics of the deities or spirits to whom the prayers are addressed. The most widely used Mapuche word for "god" is *ñunechen*, and "heaven" is generally rendered as *wenumapu*. Benevolent deities are often identified by a complimentary prefix, as in the case of *chau* ("father") *ñunechen*, or *küme* ("good") *ñunechen*, and are supposed to live in the sky; whereas malevolent supernatural agents

[16] See Figure 9, the Huaiquian-Paineo field near house No. 25.

[17] Much material has been published on this topic. The principal works are conveniently listed in Cooper, 1946, pp. 742–43. A good account by a native is given in Moesbach, 1930, pp. 371–94.

are likely to be called *wesa* ("bad") *ñunechen*, and are said to dwell in volcanoes.[18] The essential dualism of Araucanian belief is thus again made evident (cf. p. 114), but it is impossible at present to determine how many gods there are or what special functions they have.

The Reverend Juan Antinao once named as benevolent deities: *Küla-añe-fücha* ("Three-face-old man"); *Wene-kuse* ("First" or "Earliest-old-woman"), possibly a metaphor for dawn; and *Ailla-mari-kon·a* ("Ninety retainers"). Beyond the vague statement that they were of help to *machis*, Antinao could not or would not elaborate on their characters or functions; and other informants were at a loss to identify them. They are here recorded only because they may provide suggestions to some future investigator.

Another problem of interpretation arises from the lack of regularity in the ritual calendar. Apparently, *ñillatun* observances, important as they are considered, are held at irregular intervals. *Loñkos*, who used to serve as genuine leaders and spokesmen for their groups, are said to have ordered these celebrations whenever their followers were in distress or were plagued by bad dreams. We are told that today the cacique of a reservation, in consultation with the male heads of families, makes the decision at will; yet some say that a reduction should sponsor a *ñillatun* regularly every three or four years. Several communities, possibly under Christian influence, have given

[18] Several writers associate *Pillañ* with catastrophic forces, Cooper (1946, pp. 747–48). But Latcham (1924, pp. 594–98 *et passim*) argued that *Pillañ* originally stood for any ancestral spirit and that *ñunechen* is the old *Pillañ* with added attributes taken from Christian teachings. The problem of Spanish-Christian influence on contemporary Araucanian religious customs raises many vexing and unsolved questions. Contrary to popular belief, the bulk of the Mapuche are neither Catholic nor Protestant. After the Spanish period, and particularly in the second half of the nineteenth century, they were neglected by all churches; and it is only since 1900 that they have again been subject to missionary activities. Consequently, it is difficult to determine whether such customs as St. John's Day celebrations (or the widespread use of crosses) are survivals of ancient Christian practices or of still older heathen customs.

up the ceremony altogether. There is no consensus, either, with respect to the appropriate time for these events, although a slight preference is noticed for dates in the fall when the moon is full.

Even on so fundamental a point as the role played by a *machi* there was no agreement among early writers: "Moesbach and Félix José took the view that the shaman had no part in the *ñillatun* rite. And Robles Rodriguez is silent on such participation. On the other hand, Guevara and Housse have presented data showing clearly that, in at least some cases, the *machi* entered intimately and actively into the *ñillatun* rite as an intermediary between the people and the Supreme Being."[19] Whatever may have been the situation in other days or other parts of Chile, it may be categorically stated that *machis* invariably play key parts in the *ñillatun* observances now held in the vicinity of Cholchol.

A further difficulty in treating of the *ñillatun* stems from the lack of standardization. Details of performance vary widely, depending on the time and place of the ceremony, the wishes and instructions of the *machi* in charge, and whether the main objective is to give thanks or plead for help. To illustrate some of the differences and to bring out the complexity of the rituals, accounts will be given of two celebrations which I had the opportunity of observing.[20]

THE ÑILLATUN AT COIGUE

On the afternoon of March 24, 1948, the Reverend Harry Donaldson and I rode horseback from Cholchol to watch a *ñillatun* ceremony at Coigue. We had been invited by Ramón Chihuaicura, who conducts the mission school in Coigue, and the occasion was rather special as a new field was to be dedicated. After resting and taking yerba maté with our host, we proceeded to the schoolroom in which there was a large, white wooden cross, inscribed in Spanish on the crossarm with a verse from Matthew 11:28. The lettering was in green, and just be-

[19] Cooper, 1946, p. 752.

[20] Contrast the general summary of events in Cooper (1946, p. 743) with the two descriptions that follow.

low the Biblical statement was painted the Mapuche word *ñillatuin* ("let us pray").[21] A few men, including Coigue's cacique, Juan Choquilaf Malikyo, were present, and Mr. Donaldson spoke briefly in Spanish on the significance of the cross. The party then proceeded to the prayer ground, carrying along the cross and a large Chilean flag.

The *ñillatun* field was simply part of an open meadow, along the western edge of which a few ramadas had been built of leaves and branches (Pl. XIII, Fig. 2). At some distance from the shelters a deep hole was dug into which the cross was implanted with the inscription facing west. Before the hole was filled several coins and some *chicha* were put in. Then the Chilean flag was placed close by (Pl. XI, Fig. 1), together with branches of cinnamon, apple, *maki*,[22] and perhaps other trees. Near at hand a ram was tied to a short stake. This collection of objects was to be the focal point of the ceremony and served as an altar. A small number of people was present, some of whom promptly placed at the foot of the altar pottery jars of *chicha* and *mudai*. Thereafter, any thirsty person drank from one of the vessels and put it back. Whenever a dog approached it was driven off, as dogs represent evil spirits and are particularly repugnant to *machis* while professionally engaged.

When the cross was in position, its donor, Chihuaicura, the cacique of Coigue, and one or two other men, bared their heads and knelt on the ground, facing east (Pl. XII, Fig. 1). While they prayed, other men with a plow and a yoke of oxen were cutting light furrows to delimit a small hockey field between the altar and the ramadas. Scarcely had they finished, when some one fetched a hard rubber ball, and half a dozen men produced sticks and engaged in a sort of impromptu match for a few minutes. The sticks were then stacked against the altar.

At five o'clock, just as the sun began to set, the dedication

[21] One should not jump to conclusions because of the obvious Christian influence on the Coigue *ñillatun*, for wooden crosses mark many old prayer grounds and cemeteries. Only a small minority of the participants in the Coigue celebration were even nominal Christians. See footnote 18.

[22] Identified in Augusta (1916, I: 85) as Mapuche *kulüñ* (*Berberis buxifolia* Lam.; family Berberidaceae).

of the field ended, and a *machi* came forward to take charge of the *ñillatun*. Since no *machi* lives at Coigue, the chief had asked a woman from a neighboring reduction to officiate. No pay is rendered on these occasions, except in the form of gifts of food. The *machi* was dressed in traditional Araucanian garb, with a neat, clean apron, a kerchief on her head, and a minimum of ornaments. There is a belief that the deities respond better to the prayers of the poor and humble. She had the appearance of a sturdy, barefooted woman of early middle age, with strong but rather handsome features. She carried a *kul·truñ* and a string of half a dozen sleigh bells. As she came up to the altar, a younger woman similarly dressed but bareheaded stood beside her with a gourd rattle in hand. Facing east toward the cross and the distant Andes, the *machi* raised the *kul·truñ* in her left hand, struck it rapidly several times, and began to intone a speedy, somewhat monotonous chant in which she called upon *Chau* ("Father") to listen to the prayers that were to come. She then thanked him for crops, animals, and other blessings, and asked for rain and continued favors in the coming season.[23] At the close of each verse the tempo of the drum beats increased rapidly and, at the signal, "Ya!" the crowd raised the shout of "Ya, ya, YAI!" Every now and then a man sounded a blast on a *trutruka* (see Pl. XI, Fig. 1.) The chant was repeated four times, (four is the sacred number of the Araucanians), and as it drew to a finish several women advanced to the altar, broke off small branches, and held them in the left hand, while one woman dipped a twig into a bowl of water and occasionally asperged all the celebrants. At this stage Chihuaicura and the other men who had dedicated the cross knelt bareheaded behind the *machi*.

When the preliminary chanting ended, a new formation was made. This consisted of several lines of men and women of all ages, wearing all sorts of native or Chilean clothes. The *machi* and her assistant stood in the center of the front row, flanked by adult women in Araucanian dress. In time to a new chant

[23] For a text of this sort, see Augusta, 1934, p. 30, No. 14.

and drum beat the entire company in closely packed ranks began to dance backward, that is, to the west, with little jumping steps, landing sometimes on both feet and sometimes alternately on one foot or the other (Pl. XII, Fig. 2). As space opened up between the front line and the altar a young boy and girl, the cacique's son and niece, respectively, appeared. Each wore a shawl, and about the forehead a headband, into which were set bits of greenery. The boy held a bamboo pole, which he occasionally straddled like a child riding a broomstick. This pair faced the assemblage opposite the *machi*, and kept time with the others. Backward and forward, in a west-east line danced all the celebrants several times, after which the same maneuver was repeated in a south-north direction. Very soon the *machi* began to roll her eyes wildly and to breathe heavily. Her entire demeanor was that of a person who is thoroughly exhausted. Every now and then she would curl her lower lip and emit a kind of whistle, but during it all she continued to sing and dance. We were told that not much more was scheduled for this day, and as it was growing dark Mr. Donaldson and I decided to ride back to Cholchol for the night.

The next morning I returned with a native teacher from the mission. Dancing was in progress in much the same fashion as on the previous evening, except that the crowd was much larger, and many women were busy preparing food at the ramadas. As we dismounted, a young man clothed in Chilean holiday garb approached and from a bowl dipped some black paint which he daubed on our cheek bones. All the participants had been similarly smeared, and I was told that this represented both a greeting and a prayer for rain. For a similar purpose, I noticed that a bit of black cloth had been affixed to the altar, and asperging was now so copious as to suggest a mimetic shower.[24]

At about one o'clock in the afternoon the *machi*, obviously

[24] *Ñillatun* ceremonies that seek rain feature black, to represent storm clouds. Those designed for the opposite purpose use white, which stands for the sun. At Coigue rain was wanted because a long drought was making fall plowing difficult.

overheated and tired, poured some water or *mudai* from a jug at the altar to the ground, took a long drink, and then sat on a small stool facing the cross. While she rested, a man began to beat with drumsticks on the *kul·truñ*, and three performers staged the famed ostrich dance, *choike purun*. At the start, a somewhat elderly little man in tattered shirt and trousers, barefooted and bareheaded, accompanied by two young men moved to a point twenty to thirty feet east of the altar, while the other celebrants grouped themselves to the west, in an informal pack about the *machi*. For the ostrich dance, the old man affixed some sleigh bells to his waist, and the younger men had leaves bound to their foreheads (Pl. XIII, Fig. 1). Across the shoulders all three held shawls in such a fashion that they could be spread or brought together by arm movements to suggest the wings of a bird. In time to the drum's beating, the ostrich men danced toward the altar, passed it counterclockwise and returned to their starting place. The dancers gestured and posed as birds, sometimes extending one foot and then the other, flipping their shawls in and out, bobbing their heads, and turning their bodies from side to side. At one point the leader, who was really sweating profusely, bent from the waist, stuck his head into a pail of water next to the altar, and raised his bottom in imitation of a drinking bird. The audience laughed loudly in appreciation of his antics.[25]

While the ostrich dancers were performing, a group of more than fifty mounted men, led by standard-bearers carrying the Chilean flag and a black cloth affixed to a pole, formed in ranks of four, and began to gallop in a wide circuit clockwise around the entire sacred area.[26] Whenever they came abreast of the altar on the east they cried, "Ya, ya, YAI!" At intervals they charged eastward up a little hill, stopped suddenly, dismounted, bared their heads, and knelt briefly in prayer. Then they would remount and resume their circuits. As the Araucanians are

[25] Manquilef (1914, p. 187) called the ostrich dance comic.

[26] Similar circuits are made on various ceremonial occasions, to keep out or frighten off evil spirits (*ibid.*, pp. 181–83). Theoretically, they should be made in multiples of four.

superb horsemen, and many wore colorful vests or ponchos, the mounted men made a highly picturesque sight. These circuits are called *awn*.

It was impossible to keep track of the number of times that the ostrich dancers came and went, or of the circuits made by the riders, but when these activities were over a dozen or so men took hockey sticks from the altar and played a short game of *chueca* in which only a single goal was scored. The sticks were then replaced and everyone prepared to eat lunch. These special events, it developed, had been ordered by the *machi*. At the invitation of the Coigue chief, all visiting males, mounted or afoot then arranged themselves in an informal line parallel to the ramadas. Starting at one end, the cacique and Ramón Chihuaicura, as well as one or two other local residents, went from man to man, shaking hands and exchanging kinship terms or greetings with each visitor. Food was then served to visiting women and children and to a few Coigue people at the shelters, but for a long time most men of the home reservation went back and forth carrying roasted meat and apple *chicha* from their ramadas to friends and kin among the masculine visitors.[27] Beef, pig, horse, and chicken were roasted on spits over open fires, and no one was allowed to go hungry. Every resident of Coigue sent meat and drink to the *machi*, who lunched at the cacique's ramada. Some wine may have been drunk but I observed only one old man who might have been intoxicated.

Following lunch there was a long rest, after which most groups partook of hard-boiled eggs with mashed chili peppers and cider as a sort of "high tea." During the recess the Coigue chief took up a *kul·truñ*, and singing in falsetto, gave a lively imitation of the *machi*'s manner of acting. Those in the near-by ramadas who could watch this performance, thoroughly enjoyed his impromptu burlesque.

When the afternoon was well advanced, the celebrants re-

[27] By Araucanian convention gifts are given to specific individuals. No shame or embarrassment is felt by any party if a cup of *chicha*, for example, is given to one member of a group, who drinks all of it while his companions do without. Those who get more than they can eat carry the surplus home.

turned to the altar, and there was another round of chanting by the *machi*, group dancing to and from the altar, mounted circuits, and more ostrich dancing. Again the emphasis seemed to continue the dominant theme of thanksgiving and supplication, but just as the rites were concluding toward sundown a climax occurred that was apparently designed as an attack on evil spirits. Up to this point the celebrants, in close ranks, had been dancing back and forth as before. Facing the main body was the young couple that advanced and withdrew in the same rhythm as the others. Soon the *machi* began to grow wilder in her singing; she pulled the kerchief from her head and allowed her hair to tumble over her face; and she jumped vigorously up and down. Suddenly she brandished a knife in her right hand and a gourd rattle in her left. She shouted and gesticulated, stabbed at the air in all directions, and pretended to charge at the dancing couple, who backed hastily away. Once she seized the *kul·truñ* that her assistant was beating and ecstatically banged it up and down on her own head. She then paused for a few moments while a man (her husband) came forth and pressed the flat blade of a knife against her body at various points, an action that was supposed to give her strength. After that she resumed her wild dance, holding the knife aloft, jumping and whirling from side to side. While the crowd shouted and the *trutruka* sounded, a dozen men took up hockey sticks and clashed them repeatedly over the *machi*'s head. By now the *machi* appeared on the verge of a collapse, and once again men on horseback performed the *awn*, riding at a gallop around the whole sacred area as the *ñillatun* came to a close.

THE ÑILLATUN AT MALALCHE

On Friday and Saturday, April 23 and 24, 1948, the people of Malalche were hosts at a *ñillatun*. We were unable to go on the first day, but from a high spot at Cautinche we could see the ramadas and smoke from the cooking fires, and we could hear an occasional shout or the sound of a *trutruka*. Early Saturday morning, my wife, Raúl González, and I, accompanied by Juan Antinao, his daughter Josephina, and his son Melinao, proceeded to Malalche.[28] A double row of ramadas stretched for nearly 100 yards, back to back. Those on one side were roofed and, as we were told, were used by local residents, while the unroofed ramadas were for visitors. We found a vacant shelter, near which Melinao unhitched the oxen, and which we used for rest during the day. Fires were lit at each ramada, and women were busy roasting meat on long iron skewers and preparing soup and other foods. We later discovered that the shelters had been pitched on the Malalche hockey ground, and that the playing field comprised the sacred area for the *ñillatun*. At the west end of the field there were a few sacred tree branches, a white banner, several bowls containing beans, peppers, and other produce, and jars of water, *chicha*, or *mudai*. This may be described as a secondary altar. About two or three hundred feet away, toward the eastern extremity of the hockey ground, was the main altar, which was made up of cinnamon and other branches, a Chilean flag, and a white banner. Jugs of liquids and small trays of seeds and grains stood at the foot of the altar, and near by a white sheep was tied to a small stake.

When we arrived the *machi* was seated on a small stool, facing the main altar (Pl. XIV, Fig. 1).[29] Beside her stood two female assistants, each one beating a *kul·truñ*, and all three chanting in time to the music. The *machi* was short and fat, dressed in the usual Mapuche manner except for a white scarf entwined in her hair ribbons, and she held a short string of sleigh bells and a sprig of cinnamon(?) in her hand. On the opposite side of the altar a group of two young women and four

[28] The women rode in an oxcart driven by Melinao (Pl. VI, Fig. 1). The rest of us walked. My wife and Raúl made independent notes of their observations and very kindly allowed me to incorporate them with my own. Later, Juan Antinao answered numerous questions to explain the meaning of many things we had noticed.

[29] We learned that this *machi* came from Cholchol where she lived in Chilean style. Many unfavorable comments were made by our friends because she did not maintain strict control of the proceedings, and because she apparently allowed herself to become drunk as the day progressed. Juan Antinao told us afterward that she had received sixty portions of roast meat and many beverages for her services.

young men danced in separate rows toward and away from the altar, in an east-west direction. One of the men carried a Chilean flag, another a white banner, and the other two straddled bamboo poles as they danced. The rhythm was at all times six-eight and fairly quick, and two *trutrukas* were occasionally sounded by players standing north and south of the altar. Among the male spectators were many who blew rhythmically but monotonously on small *pifullkas*.

Shortly after noon the *machi* began a vigorous dance, once striking an inverted *kul·truñ* against her head. From her position west of the altar she moved north and then east, thus approaching the six young dancers, whom she appeared violently to oppose. Her assistants spat on the ground and repeatedly asperged the group of dancers. Soon the *machi* dropped to her knees and continued to dance wildly around the altar. She paused for a moment while an assistant bound a dark kerchief over her head and then, even though blindfolded, she resumed her forceful dance around the altar on her knees. When she returned to the west side, a number of men clashed hockey sticks over her head, and one man waved a knife about. The *machi* then began a conversation with an interlocutor, in the same fashion as in a *machitun* or curing service. Juan Antinao said later that her first words were, "I have come," referring to the arrival of the spirit that had possessed her. After an exchange of conventional greetings, the *machi* went on to give instructions for the successful conduct of the *ñillatun*, ordering, among other things, an ostrich dance, circuits of mounted men, and the sacrifice of a sheep. She also told the assemblage that the Araucanians were having trouble because they had given up their ancient ways. This must have sounded strange coming from a *machi* who lived in a Chilean town. When the spirit's report was finished, the *machi*'s head was uncovered and after she had rested a bit, the interlocutor reported the full conversation he had held with her.

A short time later, three young men, one very reluctantly, prepared to do the ostrich dance. Except for the use of shawls over outstretched arms they made little pretense at costuming or bird mimicry. In rather perfunctory fashion they danced eastward toward the altar and back again four(?) times. Meanwhile, a large contingent of mounted men, with standard-bearers in the front rank, lined up in rows of four and began to gallop around the prayer ground in the characteristic style of the *awn*. Several of the men blew on *pifullkas* as they went, but the riders did not keep their ranks even and made a ragged impression.

At about one o'clock in the afternoon, when the two girls and four boys had resumed their dancing forward and back, a man with a knife came from the crowd of watchers, the sheep was untied and led to the altar, and the man slit its throat and skillfully skinned and cut it up. The blood was caught in a pan, and afterward disposed of in running water so that no dog could get it, and the sheepskin was hung on the altar.

Next, the *machi* and her assistants rose, while the bystanders lined up in closely packed ranks and began to dance to and away from the altar. People of all ages and both sexes were tightly pressed together and, to add to the confusion, men on horseback mingled with those on foot. After a few formations in several directions the dancing stopped and all went to lunch. Again, as at Coigue, masculine visitors were invited to form a line and were first greeted and then fed by men of the sponsoring reservation.

There was a long rest after lunch, and the sun was beginning to set when the mass dancing started once more, with the *machi* and her assistants in the front line (Pl. XIV, Fig. 2). This time the group went the length of the hockey field from the main altar at the east to the secondary altar at the west. At one point Juan Antinao remarked that this represented a symbolic sowing of the playing ground. A very tentative suggestion is that this may indicate that hockey, which was once connected with war, is coming to be associated, as is elsewhere the case, with agriculture.

Daylight was fading when the ceremony ended and we started

back for Cautinche. Before we left, however, knots of men could be seen taking long swigs of wine from bottles brought to the spot by bootleggers.

COMPARISON OF ÑILLATUN AT COIGUE AND MALALCHE

To indicate the many variations of the *ñillatun* performance, let us now summarize the major differences in the two events just described. In contrast to Coigue, no cross was in evidence at Malalche, and while the celebration took place on a hockey field, no game of *chueca* was played. The *machi* at Malalche had two assistants and became possessed, but she lacked the poise and control of the *machi* who conducted the Coigue rites with a single assistant and without speaking in a spirit voice. The sheep staked near the Coigue altar was not sacrificed. At Malalche, there were more special dancers, more *trutrukas* and *pifullkas*, two altars, and a longer dance ground, but there was much less asperging, a poorer ostrich performance, a ragged *awn*, and far less fervor in keeping dogs away from the main altar. Furthermore, black standards and cheek marks featured the Coigue ceremony that sought rain, whereas the Malalche rites came after the winter wheat was sown and asked for sunshine by the use of white banners. Finally, there were many more participants at Malalche, and much more evidence of disorder and intoxication than was seen at Coigue.

Two features, sometimes associated with the rites, were absent both at Coigue and Malalche. One of these, *konchotun*, is called by Moesbach an annex to the *ñillatun*.[30] This is the ceremony, involving the consumption of a sacrificed sheep, by which two sets of people may pledge friendship or make matrimonial alliances. The other trait that was missing was clowning by men in masks. As explained by Juan Antinao, clowns, *ayekan wentrus*, used to be privileged performers, and their favorite trick was to snatch roasting meat away from the fire of an unwary woman. Clowning seems to have had the dual purpose of amusing spectators and of providing a happy atmos-

[30] Moesbach, 1930, p. 371.

phere so pleasing to the gods that they would be more likely to grant the prayers of the people.[31]

Irrespective of differences in details, both sets of observances were patterned along similar lines. In each case it was evident that the *ñillatun* is a complex performance, containing elements of the major Araucanian ceremonial activities. Within its structure there are included features of the public assembly (*kawiñ*), hockey game (*palikantun*), and curing ritual (*machitun*). There is a likelihood that the lack of systematization and standardization may reflect the breakdown of Mapuche social organization, but such a hypothesis can only be stated tentatively at the present time.

[31] A wide variety of songs used by masked clowns is published in Guevara 1934, pp. 322–31.

THE CHANGING PATTERN OF CULTURE

MUCH that has been written in the preceding pages provides ample evidence that Araucanian culture is in a state of flux. Dynamic forces impinge on every aspect of Mapuche life, and the people betray uncertainty and uneasiness as they find themselves increasingly called upon to give up the ways of the past and to conform to conditions of the present. By way of recapitulation and conclusion a review and analysis will be given of some of the salient features of the process that is bringing about the changing pattern of Araucanian culture. The forces of change do not, it is evident, operate independently in isolated segments of culture, but interconnect and interact on each other at all times. For purposes of analysis it occasionally becomes necessary to disentangle some of the elements concerned and to discuss them separately, but wherever possible an attempt will be made to treat each aspect of change within a broad cultural context. The earlier phases of Araucanian history will be disregarded and the warring period in the nineteenth century in which a strong patrilineate prevailed will serve as a point of departure. Attention will be focused on the changes that have taken place since pacification and reservation life began.

It would not be hard to show that in the realm of material things the principal effects have been a loss of traditional arts and crafts and the substitution, wherever circumstances allowed, of Spanish-Chilean products, raw materials, and styles. Changes of house type and costume have been noted earlier, and attention was called to the greater conservatism of women in matters of dress. Abandonment of native industries is not, however, a simple matter of recognizing and accepting the greater utility and convenience of modern gadgets. Not only did the old system of handicrafts provide satisfying work for many artisans, but methods for distributing the finished products were adjusted to the rest of the socioeconomic structure. Today, one either pays for a trade object in cash or does without. Yet the Araucanians have not developed the concept of money, and their opportunities to acquire cash are exceedingly limited. As a group they have so little purchasing power that they are merely on the outer fringe of the Chilean financial system. The government lacks the resources to subsidize the Indians in any way whatsoever, and private manufacturers and traders can find little reason for making concessions to such poor customers. Consequently, the natives who cannot buy the things they need are discouraged and dispirited, and the shift in material culture has serious ramifications that result, at least for the time being, in a lowering of efficiency and morale.

Another aspect of transition that has a material base but extends into other areas of culture is the matter of drunkenness. Reverend Juan Antinao repeatedly affirmed: "Alcoholism is the curse of the Mapuche." No doubt he was influenced by Christian teachings, but there is much point to his statement in sociologic terms. In times past when a man became drunk, he was among friends and relatives at home or on a friendly reservation. He did not pay money for his liquor, nor did he put into jeopardy much more than his own health and comfort. Nowadays the pattern of drunkenness tends to run along different lines. The favorite drinks are not "home brews" of one sort or another but cheap wines sold in every town and city at numerous establishments that operate with or without legal license. To buy liquor one must pay cash, and when the craving is sufficiently strong a man will resort to all kinds of practices to get funds. He may sell bits of needed equipment, stores of seed or food, standing crops, or unborn animals, and he may even turn to thievery and robbery. Furthermore, while intoxicated, he may go so far as to dispose of his land, a contingency that could not have arisen in the old days.

A typical example of what may befall a drunken man concerns one of my informants who, in his youth, went into Cholchol with a cart drawn by two fine oxen and loaded with wheat to be milled. He remembers having had a few drinks. The next day, he woke up half-naked under a bridge. Gone were his cart, his wheat, and his bullocks. Similar tales are told of other men. Many people deplore such a state of affairs, but even some of the more realistic missionaries who are struggling to introduce temperance admit that drunkenness provides a measure of escape for men whose lives are drab and unrewarding.

Much of the sense of futility arises from one of the most far-reaching of all aspects of culture change, the loss of one scheme of values and the slowness or failure to develop a new one. Under the former social system a man had numerous opportunities to gain prestige and esteem by excelling in battle or by showing great skill at hockey and other strenuous exercises. If he had the resourcefulness and initiative to acquire several wives, he usually begot numerous offspring and had enough females in his household to raise his food, cater to his comfort, and show the deference due to the head of a family. Should he, in addition, exhibit a forceful character and a vigorous manner of speech, he might become a *werken;* and if he combined these qualities with the paternity of many sons he had a fair chance of becoming a *loñko*. At present the old incentives and rewards for masculine ambition are gone, and no new mechanisms for achieving and exhibiting high status have been devised to take their place. No honors are to be won by diligent farming, and to be thrifty and to make or save money likewise arouses little interest, except among those who are willing to imitate and compete with Chileans.

Equally effective in lowering Araucanian morale has been the transition from occupancy of more than ample territory with abundant natural resources to confinement on strictly limited reservation lands the potentials of which are steadily decreasing. There was a time when, in the event of internal tension, an enterprising man could strike out into a virgin area and found a new settlement. Today, this sort of "safety valve" is no longer available. Men who hold titles in severalty gain a small measure of independence and autonomy, but they are tied down for life. When they become extremely unhappy in their relations with housemates or neighbors, they have only two means of escape. They may wander away to Argentina, or they may look for jobs in a town or on a private estate. In either case the individual must be prepared to become a sort of displaced person, and must try to adjust himself to a new cultural setting in which he is unlikely to rise very high. The number of dispossessed Araucanians who, for one reason or another, have become laborers on lands owned by others is already large enough to suggest a nascent system of peonage.

Coupled with the social and economic restrictions imposed by reservation life and the allotment program is the disintegration of the political structure. Chieftainship under former conditions derived much of its strength from a leader's control of his band's land, as well as from the size and fidelity of his following. Patrilocal and unilocal residence gave each unit a sense of stability and physical cohesion and made easy the implementation of political loyalties by the device of frequent councils at which each man could speak his mind. Bonds of attachment were forged at assemblies at which the retainers of one or two friendly *loñkos* ate, drank, sang, danced, gossiped, and made love. There was a comforting sense of belonging to a particular group, and outsiders were looked upon with suspicion as potential enemies or witches. When death occurred and threatened the stability of a band, the surviving members rallied around to prevent further harm by pacifying the soul of the deceased with a suitable funeral and by taking pains to discover and punish the disloyal person (witch) who had caused the death. Chiefs were expected to be on the alert to protect their followers by detecting and weeding out sorcerers, and they could be ruthless in killing or expelling those who were judged guilty. In other ways, too, caciques were responsible for maintaining group harmony. They had to organize their men into fighting units, keep polygyny within bounds but so equitably distributed that no one grew resentful or rebellious, see that each man had sufficient land to supply his wants, and serve as judges in the settlement of whatever disputes arose. Moreover, a *loñko* was expected to supervise the training of his retainers' children, and through his *werkens* to keep up good relations with other chiefs who would stand him in good stead if ever he needed the support of allies. There is a suggestion that *loñkos* were once reinforced in their authority by supernatural sanctions, and Latcham may well be correct in claiming that group ceremonies used to be led by caciques.

At present every aspect of chieftainship has been drastically modified. Whatever native leadership the people still have is so vaguely defined as to be of little importance. As long as men hold individual titles to their land and its usufruct, they do not need to rely on a *loñko* to tell them when or where to farm. They find it equally unnecessary to seek his advice on the disposition of their crops or other goods, or to consult him in regard to marriage. Disputes are not referred to a cacique for settlement, nor can any leader order suspected sorcerers to be punished or expelled. Chilean courts have the same jurisdiction over Araucanians that they have over other nationals; there is a police station in each town; and the carabineros have the right of investigation and arrest on any reservation within their territory. In practice, the police seldom interfere in the internal affairs of the Mapuche, and those natives who resort to government courts are rarely pleased with the treatment they receive. As is so true elsewhere, litigation in Chile is apt to be expensive and long drawn out. Complaints of unfairness are often heard, and the phrase, "there is no justice," is frequently repeated. The Ministerio de Tierras y Colonización maintains an office in Temuco over which presides a judge of Indian affairs. Court is held about three days a week, and crowds of natives come in from outlying districts. Almost inevitably, they seek adjustment of land titles. If they can establish their identity and show that they have an authentic claim, they generally get a legal document of ownership, but this court only confirms previously assigned holdings and does not allot new land or grant titles to other than presumed heirs of previous owners. Incredible confusion arises from the Mapuche custom of duplicating names, from failures of men to list all their wives and offspring, and from the lack of accurate records. Even the wisest and best intentioned of judges must, inevitably, make numerous mistakes, and the natives often leave the courtroom feeling that they can get no justice from the government or from their own leaders.

Religious functions, too, have passed out of the hands of the chiefs. True, they may exercise discretion in setting a date for an assembly or *ñillatun*, and they may select an officiating *machi* and other participants, but once the rites get under way a *loñko* has little more to do than any other celebrant.

All in all, the bonds of loyalty to a chief, the sentiments of attachment to one's own group, and the ties of kinship and common residence that served to give each community a sense of cohesion and solidarity have virtually disappeared. Members of a reduction may still show a bit of neighborly interest in one another and, to some degree, relationship ties may hold together coresidents of a reservation that was founded by a close kinship group, but growing schisms and factionalism are everywhere apparent, and community enterprises have been reduced to the joint sponsorship of an occasional assembly, *ñillatun*, or hockey game, or else to a show of common interest in the maintenance of a school.

Schooling, in turn, has become a prime agent in facilitating the breakdown of Araucanian culture. Not only is instruction conveyed in a foreign tongue (Spanish), but most of the available schools are conducted by missionaries. Rural schools, especially, are taught by Christianized natives. This means that much time is devoted to preaching and hymn singing, and that values and virtues not based on Mapuche life are taught. Then, too, the missions customarily offer far better medical care than the state provides, and with every cure by doctor, nurse, or trained missionary, the people's confidence in *machis* grows less and less. Just the same, and regardless of how much parents may regret the passing of the old order, the great majority of them are practical enough to recognize the advantages of education and to encourage their youngsters to get as much schooling as possible. Already the young folk excel their elders in arithmetic, speaking, reading, and writing Spanish, and as time goes on more and more of them are adopting Chilean ways. The relationship of schooling to Christianity and the speeding up of acculturation were vividly impressed on me not only at the mission station in Cholchol, but also when I visited a small rural school at Malalche, in the company of Juan Antinao. Part of the one-room building had folding doors, behind which were an altar and other furnishings of a chapel. Reverend Antinao greeted the teacher, introduced me to her and to the class, then spoke to the pupils in Spanish, praising their Chilean "brothers" and urging them to learn to be good Chileans.

It is important to realize that the weight of cultural readjustment has fallen unequally on the two sexes. Men have been much more completely deprived of their former means of achieving status than have women. It might even be argued that the lot of women has in some ways been improved since pacification. No new cares of any significance have been added to their age-old duties, they have been released from most of the farming responsibilities, and those who have had schooling are developing a spirit of independence that was formerly lacking. The most important and sacred of the ceremonies still performed are entrusted to female *machis*, and few are the men who treat their spouses as chattels. In more than one instance I was impressed with the scrupulous care taken by husbands to avoid offering for sale articles that belonged to their wives. When journeys are being made women do not trudge afoot with burdens on their backs, but sit in carts while the menfolk walk or serve as drivers. Nor is it easy to forget a scene in Temuco's main plaza in which a Mapuche woman publicly and shrilly abused a man who lowered his head and hurriedly crossed the street to escape her loud nagging. It would be a mistake, however, to think that women enjoy full equality with men. On the reservations they continue to cater to their menfolk and exhibit marked signs of respect, and in the towns it is a common sight to see a woman waiting mournfully in an oxcart outside a wineshop, while her husband drinks up the money she had planned to put to other use.

A number of social maladjustments have arisen from population changes resulting from the cessation of warfare, together with the decline of preferential cross-cousin marriage. During the years when losses in battle served to keep down the proportion of males to females, and while polygyny permitted each man to have several spouses, there was little danger of adults remaining unwed. Furthermore, observance of cross-cousin marriage, together with sororate and levirate practices, regularized and simplified the selection of spouses. Nowadays, young adult men and women exercise more independence in the choice of mates, but marriage is no longer the more or less automatic social mechanism that it once was. Lack of land or other sources of income keeps many a young man from taking a wife, and this economic deterrent, together with the abandonment of polygyny, has led to a greater proportion of spinsters despite the increased percentage of men in the population. Without the levirate and filial inheritance of spouses, too, an ever-mounting number of widows are finding it harder to rewed and must achieve some other way of supporting themselves and their minor children. Whether the increase of unwed people has led to more frequent prostitution and irregular sexual conduct is hard to establish, but this may well be the case.

One of the most important attributes brought about by the changing pattern of Araucanian culture has been the development of a deep sense of shame, whereas the Mapuche used to be noted for arrogance and attitudes of superiority in dealing with outsiders. The sense of shame and a consequent shyness of behavior are most noticeable in the reluctance to invite white people to their houses for meals. This might be wrongly attributed to a lack of hospitality. For instance, although we were almost never asked to dine in native homes, we were constantly sent gifts of food. In the same connection, few people would accept invitations to eat with us in the caravan, although male visitors were generally willing to take a cup of tea or coffee. On one occasion Mrs. Antinao, who was forever doing us thoughtful favors, such as bringing dry straw for starting the fire on rainy mornings, was persuaded to take tea with my wife. She seemed very happy to have a chance to chat and to inspect the furnishings of the caravan, but at the same time she kept a wary eye out for me and hurried away the moment I appeared.

Feelings of shame are most apt to be aroused at those points at which the Indians are aware that they diverge most widely from accepted Chilean norms. Contemporary Araucanians realize that many people condemn them as ignorant, poor, dirty, shiftless, drunken, and lazy, partly because they have different forms of behavior and outlook. Yet the Mapuche have a nostalgic regard for many of their traditional practices and are unwilling to give them up altogether. Consequently, one detects uncertainty and a marked ambivalence in their attitudes. Sometimes they seem ready to forego native customs and become thoroughly assimilated, but at other times they try to resist the pressure to change. For example, even those who recognize the greater efficacy of medical science, may hesitate to forego the ministrations of a *machi*. Within a broader frame of reference the matter of land ownership is a case in point. The Mapuche may not like the current system of being forced to live on fixed reservations, yet most of them realize that this very system gives them a measure of protection, and that their way of life would be much more likely to be lost in competition with Chilean customs if their lands were not set aside as reservations.

A final review of Araucanian culture in transition throws light on several important characteristics of cultural dynamics. As in any study of dynamics, it is a matter of analyzing a balance of forces, in this case forces of sociocultural change versus forces of inertia. Not all the former press with equal intensity on all sectors of a given social structure, nor are they always resisted with equal strength. With regard to the Mapuche it is obvious that pacification and the attendant loss of symbolic masculine values gained through boldness and fighting ability have had a far more drastic effect than the introduction of new styles of dress or housing and that resistance to changes in material culture has been less steady than the reluctance to accept basic Christian teachings. Then, again, it should be noted that changes originating in one sphere of activity are likely to spread into other areas of the culture pattern. Thus, ownership of reservation land in severalty begins as a material and economic shift but can be shown to exert a powerful influence on chieftainship and marriage customs.

As the forces of change continue to manifest themselves people grow hesitant and uncertain and often become dispirited and maladjusted. While their morale is at low ebb feelings of shame are apt to arise, especially when they contrast their situation with that of a neighboring group which appears to possess greater stability and self-assurance. Nevertheless, the sense of shame does not necessarily engender complete willingness to abandon traditional customs. The net result is a series of compromises whereby old traits are modified rather than lost or replaced by totally new ones. Specifically, not every Mapuche lives in an old-style, thatched *ruka*, yet other kinds of houses are in a distinct minority, and even frame houses are likely to be straw covered so that they resemble *rukas*. Nearly all women regularly wear modern aprons and blouses, yet a woman entirely dressed in an old-fashioned costume is no rare sight, and combinations of native and Chilean garments are very common. Some new varieties of food and drink are not infrequently consumed, but there is still a marked taste for Mapuche bread and for native beverages such as *mudai*. Although aboriginal arts and crafts have almost disappeared, enough craftsmen remain active to keep most households supplied with basketry trays, wooden spoons and bowls, handwoven ponchos and blankets, and old-style ornaments and musical instruments. Polygyny is unquestionably fading out, but men with multiple wives may yet be found on most reservations. Mapuche religion which, apparently, was never strongly organized, is slowly yielding to missionary pressure, and medical science is gradually replacing shamanistic practices; but a host of pagan beliefs survive, and *machis* are still called upon to effect cures and officiate at *ñillatuns*. Hockey has lost its former significance for training warriors, but as a competitive sport it is highly popular and much esteemed. Education along new lines and the use of Spanish are being widely accepted as a part of modern Araucanian life, but it is most significant that no segment of the old culture has been more completely preserved than the use of the Mapuche language. Every man, woman, and child that claims to be an Indian has a fluent command of Mapuche no matter how acculturated he may be in other respects.

Above all, it is apparent that the process of culture change is slow, nonsymmetrical, all-pervasive, and cumulative. It operates not so much by the sudden displacement or elimination of established traits, as by means of a series of successive modifications. After powerful forces of change have once been generated, they cannot easily be dissipated before they have run their full course, even if the people affected are made unhappy and ashamed in the interim. Inertia may slow down the process somewhat, but in the end enough trait alterations are effectuated to make the traditional culture unrecognizable. So, the Araucanians may yet retain some of their old ways of life for a few generations, but a time will inevitably come when their former usages will persist only as memories.

LITERATURE CITED

AUGUSTA, FÉLIX JOSÉ DE

1916 Diccionario araucano, I Araucano-español, II Español-araucano. Santiago de Chile: Imprenta Universitaria.

1934 Lecturas araucanas. 2d ed.; Padre las Casas: Imprenta "San Francisco."

BRAND, DONALD D.

1941*a* A Brief History of Araucanian Studies. N. Mex. Anthropol., V, No. 2: 19–35.

1941*b* The Status of Anthropology in Chile. *Ibid.*, No. 3: 55–71.

1941*c* The Peoples and Languages of Chile. *Ibid.*, No. 3: 72–93.

COOPER, JOHN M.

1946 The Araucanians. Handbook of South American Indians. ed. Julian H. Steward. Washington: Smithson. Instit., II: 687–760.

DUGAN, W. H.

1937 Hacia una solución de la problema del terreno araucano. La Aurora araucana. (This journal was published irregularly by the Anglican Misión Araucana between 1936 and 1939.)

EDWARDS, AUGUSTÍN

1929 Peoples of Old. London: E. Benn, Ltd.

1930 Gentes de Antaño. Valparaiso: Soc. Imprenta y Lithographia Universo.

FONTECILLA, L. ARTURO

1946 La Platería entre los Araucanos. Rev. chilena de hist. y geogr. Santiago, No. 107: 247–71.

GALDAMES, LUIS

1941 A History of Chile (trans. I. J. Cox). Chapel Hill: Univ. N. Carolina Press.

GRAHAM, ROBERT B. C.

1927 Pedro de Valdivia. New York and London: Harper & Brothers.

GUEVARA, S. TOMÁS

1898 Historia de la civilización de Araucanía. Anal. Univ. Santiago de Chile.

1908 Psicolojia del pueblo araucano. Santiago de Chile: Imprenta Cervantes.

1911 Folklore araucano. Santiago de Chile: Imprenta Cervantes.
1929 Historia de Chile: Chile prehispano, I and II. Santiago de Chile: Balcells & Co.

HALLOWELL, A. IRVING
1943 Araucanian Parallels to the Omaha Kinship Pattern. Amer. Anthropol., XLV: 489–91.

HILGER, M. INEZ
1946 Ethnological Field Study of the ... Training of the Araucanian Indian Child of Chile. *In* Year Book Amer. Phil. Soc., pp. 202–5.

HOUSSE, R. ÉMILE
1939 Une Epopée indienne: les araucans du Chili. Paris: Plon.
1940 Epopeya India (R. P. Andres Goy, trans.). Santiago de Chile: Empresa Editoria Zig-Zag.

JEFFERSON, MARK
1921 Recent Colonization in Chile. Amer. Geog. Soc., Research Ser. No. 6. New York: Oxford Univ. Press.

JOSEPH, H. CLAUDE
1931*a* La Vivienda araucana. Santiago de Chile: Balcells & Co.
1931*b* Los Tejidos araucanos. Padre los Casas: Imprenta "San Francisco."
1933–34 Costumbres araucanas. Rev. Universitaria, Univ. Católica de Chile, Nos. 5 and 6, 1933, pp. 705–16; No. 4, 1934, pp. 517–28.

LATCHAM, RICHARD E.
1909 Ethnology of the Araucanos, Journ. Royal Anthropol. Instit., XXXIX: 334–70.
1924 La Organización social y las creencias religiosas de los antiguos araucanos. Publ. mus. etnol. y antropol. Chile, III, Nos. 2, 3, 4: 245–868.

LESSER, ALEXANDER
1929 Kinship Origins in the Light of Some Distributions. Amer. Anthropol., XXXI: 710–30.

LOTHROP, SAMUEL K.
1930 Notes on Indian Textiles of Central Chile. Indian Notes, Mus. Amer. Indian. Heye Foundation, VII, No. 3: 324–35.
1945 Richard E. Latcham 1869–1943. Amer. Anthropol., XLVII, No. 4: 603–8.

Lowie, Robert H.
1929 Culture and Ethnology. New York: P. Smith.
Manquilef, Manuel
1914 Comentarios del pueblo araucano, II, La Jimnasia nacional. Anal. Univ. Chile, Rev. folklore chileno, XXXIV.
McBride, George M.
1936 Chile: Land and Society. Amer. Geogr. Soc., Res. Ser., No. 19.
Métraux, Alfred
1939 Le Shamanisme araucan. Rev. instit. antropol. univ. nac. Tucumán, II No. 1: 309–62.
Moesbach, Ernesto W. de
1930 Vida y costumbres de los indígenas araucanos en la segunda mitad del siglo XIX. Santiago: Imprenta Cervantes.
Molina, Juan I.
1808 The Geographical, Natural and Civil History of Chili (trans. by an American gentleman). Middletown, Conn.: I. Riley.
Murdock, George P.
1949 Social Structure. New York: Macmillan Co.
Oyarzún, Aureliano
1917 Cay-Cay y Ten-Ten. Publ. mus. etnol. y antropol. Chile, I, Pt. 2: 119–27.
Oyarzún, Aureliano, and Richard E. Latcham
1928 Album de tejidos y alferería araucana. Santiago: Mus. etnol. antropol.
Robles, Eulojio R.
1912 Costumbres i creencias araucanas. Anal. univ. Chile, Rev. folklore chileno, CXXX: 155–81.
Smith, Edmond R.
1855 The Araucanians. New York: Harper & Brothers.
Soustelle, Georgette and Jacques
1938 Folklore chilien. Paris: Instit. internat. de coopération intellectuelle.
Titiev, Mischa
1943 The Influence of Common Residence on the Unilateral Classification of Kindred. Amer. Anthropol., XLV, No. 4.
1944 Old Oraibi: a Study of the Hopi Indians of Third Mesa.

Papers Peabody Mus. Amer. Archaeol. and Ethnol., XXII, No. 1.
1949 Social Singing among the Mapuche Anthropol. Papers Mus. Anthropol., Univ. Mich., No. 2.

TREUTLER, PABLO
1861 La Provincia de Valdiviai los araucanos. Santiago: Imprenta chilena.

WHITE, LESLIE A.
1939 A Problem in Kinship Terminology. Amer. Anthropol., XLI, No. 4: 566–73.

INDEX

PLATE I

FIG. 1. Young boy driving an oxcart.

FIG. 2. Little boys with oxen raking a newly plowed field.

PLATE II

FIG. 1. The framework of a *ruka* under construction.

(Rudy Hirsch photograph)

FIG. 2. A baby tied in its cradleboard.

PLATE III

FIG. 1. Backing the caravan into place at Cautinche.

FIG. 2. Reverend Juan Antinao with his wife and five of their children.

PLATE IV

FIG. 1. Children playing *chueca* in the schoolyard at Cautinche. From the entrance of the caravan.

FIG. 2. Women wearing traditional Araucanian costumes. The pompons worn by the younger women are commonly used on festive occasions.

PLATE V

FIG. 1. Winter travel. The main highway linking Cholchol with the rail center at Nueva Imperial, at the height of the rainy season.

FIG. 2. Crossing the Cholchol River at Los Boldos. Passengers and crew haul on the steel cable at the left of the raft.

PLATE VI

FIG. 1. A journey by oxcart from Cautinche to Malalche. The party is en route to the *ñillatun* at Malalche.

FIG. 2. The first plane landing at Cholchol. Indians and Chileans nearly obscure the small airplane that marks the end of the "oxcart age."

PLATE VII

FIG. 1. The home of the *machi* at Cautinche. Her nonprofessional status is indicated by the absence of a *rewe*. Only the poles in the middle ground reveal her calling.

FIG. 2. The home of a Carrarriñe *machi*. The *rewe*, surmounted by twigs of sacred trees, is set at an angle before the *ruka*.

PLATE VIII

(Rudy Hirsch photograph)

A *machi* climbing her *rewe*. The *machi* holds a *kul·truñ* and drumstick. Her *kul·truñ* is decorated with traditional markings.

PLATE IX

FIG. 1. A male *machi* and two assistants. The one at the left holds a small gourd rattle in each hand. J. M. Collío identified the *machi* as a hermaphrodite nicknamed Alamo.

FIG. 2. Juan Leviu ("Sekuta") Paineo playing a *llollkin* of his own make at Carrarriñe. The pail of water enabled him to clear his instrument.

PLATE X

Fig. 1. A *machi's* grave in the Malalche cemetery.

Fig. 2. The original cemetery at Cautinche. Although no Christian was ever buried here, the entrance is marked with a cross.

PLATE XI

FIG. 1. Dedication of a new cross at Coigue. A *ñillatun* field is being inaugurated. The donor of the cross is in white shirt sleeves at the left of the second row. The officiating *machi* faces the group, and a *trutruka* player is at the left. A Chilean flag, a black standard, and jars of *mudai* and *chicha* are next to the cross.

FIG. 2. The principal *ñillatun* field at Carrarriñe. The same area is used for hockey.

PLATE XII

FIG. 1. Start of the *ñillatun* at Coigue. The worshippers kneel and the *machi* stands ready with her *kul·truñ* poised. Coigue's cacique, the little man leaning forward in the front row, is about to asperge the gathering with a twig from a bowl of water.

FIG. 2. Progress of the *ñillatun* at Coigue. The dancers are moving backward away from the altar. The *machi*, in a long white apron, stands in the middle of the front row.

PLATE XIII

FIG. 1. Two ostrich dancers at Coigue. The distinctive aspects of the costumes are the shawls over their shoulders and the headbands of leaves.

FIG. 2. Ramadas at Coigue. The women prepare food while the *ñillatun* is in progress.

PLATE XIV

FIG. 1. Main altar of the *ñillatun* at Malalche.

FIG. 2. Dance group at Malalche. The dancers are approaching the main altar. The *machi* is the short, stout woman in a light apron, second to the right from the woman holding a baby. The disordered appearance of the group is noteworthy.

PLATE XV

FIG. 1. The family of Segundo Paineo at Carrarriñe, in front of a storehouse, by the *ruka* in which they live. The boy at the left is the son of Mrs. Paineo's brother.

FIG. 2. Hockey game at Carrarriñe. Players and spectators wear everyday clothes. Fermin Collío stands left of center, with his feet spread wide apart.

PLATE XVI

FIG. 1. Two men from Renaco. Fermin Nahuelhual, the cacique (left), and Segundo Huenchual. Although Segundo regards himself as an Araucanian his face shows little evidence of Indian ancestry.

FIG. 2. Children at Carrarriñe. Behind them is the one-room school conducted by the Misión Araucana. Domingo Carilaf, the teacher, is at the extreme right.